POETIC VOYAGES
SURREY VOL II

Edited by Dave Thomas

First published in Great Britain in 2001 by
YOUNG WRITERS
Remus House,
Coltsfoot Drive,
Peterborough, PE2 9JX
Telephone (01733) 890066

HB ISBN 0 75433 388 4
SB ISBN 0 75433 389 2

FOREWORD

Young Writers was established in 1991 with the aim to promote creative writing in children, to make reading and writing poetry fun.

This year once again, proved to be a tremendous success with over 88,000 entries received nationwide.

The Poetic Voyages competition has shown us the high standard of work and effort that children are capable of today. It is a reflection of the teaching skills in schools, the enthusiasm and creativity they have injected into their pupils shines clearly within this anthology.

The task of selecting poems was therefore a difficult one but nevertheless, an enjoyable experience. We hope you are as pleased with the final selection in *Poetic Voyages Surrey Vol II* as we are.

CONTENTS

Bramley School

Georgina Hewett	22
Katie Caddick	23
Hannah Patrick	23
Harriet Hewett	24
Ruth Connick	24
Aimee King	24
Camilla Barden	25
Susannah Fownes	25
Madeleine Kuhler	26
Sophie Gribben	26
Olivia Naylor	27
Emily Owen	28
Charlotte Wearn & Stephanie Young	28
Danniella Schindler	29
Jenny Shanks	30
Charlotte Bloodworth	30
Lucy Houlding	31
Amy Wildgoose	31
Laura McLean	32
Bethany Wardle	32
Rebecca Rainback & Alice Boulding	33
Clare Bushell	33
Emily Howard	34
Sarah Muggleton	34
Katie Buckhalter	35
Lauren Morton	35
Sophie Grice	36
Nicola Taylor	36
Natasha Ward	37
Susannah Long	37
Emily Eason	38
Sarah Phillips	38

Broomfield House School

Sydney White	39
Phoebe Small	39

Charlotte Owen	40
Francesca Miller	40
Polly Kemp-King	41
Emma Robson	41
Natalie York	42
Kate Hare	42
Rosalind Gealy	43
Alex Dass	43
Oliver Burman	44
Oliver Turner	44

Byfleet Primary School

Sam Colgate	45
Megan Parry	46
Kimberley Oxborough	46
Lucy O'Leary	47
Stephen Braine	48
Melissa Warner	48
Sam Royston	49
Lauren White	50
Alex Doune	50
Caitlin Powell	51
Daniel Axten-Jones	52
Matthew Ogbourn	53
Tia Render	54

Cuddington Community Primary School

Luca Sepe	55
Pierre Timms	55
Jievagan Bala	56
Daniel Mills	56
Lauren Marks	57
Hayley Copland	57
Michael Niven	58
Hayley Randall	59
Chloe Bissell	60

Nicholas Hammond	82
Hayley Evans	82
Anna Sanders	83
Samual Brant	84
Victoria Filshie	85
Louise Cooper	86
Andrew Warrender	87
Ben May	87
Roxanne Brunswick	88
Natalie Watkinson	88
Lisa Patterson	89
David Barlow	89
Catherine Rogers	90
Natalie Logan	90
James Uphill	91
Katie Lemon	91
Stephanie Roberts	92
Pennie Glassup	92
Lara Berriman	93
Joshua Brant	93
Suzy Fenge	94
Alice Surey	94
Danny Wheeler	95
Corrinne Padwick	95

St Ann's Heath Junior School, Virginia Water

Nathalie Davy	95
Katie Neck	96
Lara Day	96
Nicola Bean	97
Anna Morrison	97
Jake McGuire	98
Isobel McNeill	98
Harriet McGuire	99
Jack Foster	99
Harry Matthews	100

Antony Capes	100
Gemma Moore	101
Fiona Everington	101
Petra Aryiku	102
Helen Moggridge	102
Michelle Green	103
Amelia Clarke	103
Katie Morris	103
Melanie Wright	104
Laura Tayler	104
Cara Vaisey	105
Sophie Clarke	105
Helen Jenkins	106
Jennifer Davy	106
Jennifer Shelley	107
Laura Dossett	107
Rebecca Bean	108
Emma Laing	108
Joy Hunt	109
Daniel Norris	109
Jonathan Miller	110
Rebecca Kelly	110
Charlotte MacKenzie	111
Hayley Hedges	111
Abigail Houghton	112
Lucy Morris	112
Levi Draper-Smith	113
Jack Milnes	113
Laura Stephens	114
Tiffany Ellson	114
BethanyHolmes	115
Hannah Maunder	115
Dominic Shine	115
Abigail Gaskin	116
Emma Graham	116
Marie Elsdon	117
Natasha Day	118

Stephanie Giles	189
Alex Romaines	190
Claire Eggar	190
Laura Sharkey	191
Rachel Garrett	191
Jamie Simmons	192
Frances Kenyon	193
Gemma Brogan	194

Warren Mead Junior School

Ben Thomas	195
Sally Fletcher	195
Christina Davis	196
Elizabeth Thompson	197
Hayley Javeleau	198
Tom Bovington	199
Sara Manaton	200

The Poems

THE CASTLE

Creaking,
An escaping prisoner on the stairs stupidly stood on a creaky stair.

Squeaking,
A petrified mouse running from a hissing cat in the hallway.

Rattling,
A brave knight running downstairs in his copper armour.

Clattering,
A fragile plate fell from a wobbly shelf in the kitchens.

Munching,
The small mouse eating some tasty biscuits.

Scrunching,
Leaves fluttering in the castle gardens.

Dripping,
A constant tap hitting the sink every second.

Sitting,
The king fell into his throne heavily.

Christie Cheesman (9)
Ashley CE Primary School

THE CASTLE

Taunting, taunting, a terrifying ghost scaring people.
Haunting, haunting, a lot of dreadful monsters being horrible.
Hissing, hissing, a witch saying an evil curse.
Kissing, kissing, the prince and princess getting married.
Squeaking, squeaking, a jet black bat hanging from the ceiling.
Creaking, creaking, an immortal prisoner on an old floorboard.

Philip Hussey (9)
Ashley CE Primary School

THE CASTLE

Moaning . . .
Sinful prisoners quietly sighing in the dark, dingy dungeons.
Groaning . . .
The fierce wind whistling through miniature gaps in the stone walls
of the dazzling living room.

Creaking . . .
The attentive footsteps of an old bent butler on the dusty wooden stairs.
Squeaking . . .
Filthy rats scurrying swiftly around in the dark, damp cellar.

Rustling . . .
Brown leaves on the large brown oak in the dark misty cellar.
Bustling . . .
The royal guests in the big bright hallway.

Sam Adam (8)
Ashley CE Primary School

THE CASTLE

Moaning . . .
The sad, white ghost playing in the massive, dark corridor.
Groaning . . .
The old grumpy maid in the smelly empty kitchen.

Sneaking . . .
Down the long steep stairs the young scary ghost child.
Creaking . . .
The old dusty floorboards in the gloomy bedroom.

Dying . . .
The grand king on his throne.
Crying . . .
Is his beautiful daughter.

Smashing . . .
The silver cutlery in the kitchen.
Crashing . . .
The two knights in the battle ring.

Hannah Hawkins (10)
Ashley CE Primary School

THE HAUNTED CASTLE

Crashing,
As the butler drops some cups.
Smashing,
As the tray falls down the stairs.
Talking,
As the old, crinkly ghost is sleeping in a coffin.
Walking,
As the tall, ancient butler takes the cups with blood on to the
dirty, bloodstained kitchen.
Rustling,
As the old, slow ghost looks for a magic spell book.
Tussling,
As the fat old king pushes a basket over.
Scratching,
As the thin creepy ghost scratches the ancient brick on the wall of the
castle.
Matching,
As the elderly, aged ghost lights a match to find his way down the dark
creaky corridor.

Kyle Malik (8)
Ashley CE Primary School

THE CASTLE OF SPOOKS

Squeaking,
A bat quietly hanging from the high ceiling.

Ticking,
The big clock in the long corridor.

Leaking,
A loud drip falling from the metal tap.

Hissing,
A sly snake out in the frosty garden.

Ringing,
The huge church bells clanging together loudly.

Screaming,
A mummy runs around like mad!
Aagghh!

Natalie Wroth (9)
Ashley CE Primary School

THE CASTLE

Crying,
A weak echoing cry of a ghost child.
Sighing,
The loud deafening sigh of a maid up in the rooms.

Smashing,
All the bright gleaming glasses in the great wintry hall of honour.
Crashing,
Rats in the dark gloomy cellar knocking over fierce potions.

Creaking,
Of mouldy old doors opening and closing one after another.
Sneaking,
A black figure with jewels from the castle going slowly
Into the dark shadowy night.

Holly Mist (9)
Ashley CE Primary School

HAUNTERS

Dripping,
The rusty breaking tap in the dark eerie bathroom.
Snipping,
The hairy nasty spider under the mouldy floor.

Moaning,
The white, strange ghost on the weird shadowy bedroom window sill
                    slowly singing.
Groaning,
The mad sinister witch in the cellar boiling.

Rustling,
The nasty horrid rats running down the steep narrow stairs chasing.
Bustling,
The tall, bloody vampire in the smoky black kitchen hurrying.

Grumbling,
The tiny green goblin in the slimy haunted cupboard dying.
Rumbling,
The huge dragon in the deep blue moat roaring.

Tapping,
The sinister glaring troll at the wooden square door waiting anxiously.
Rapping,
The quiet cat catching the grey fat mice.

Helen Spencer (8)
Ashley CE Primary School

IN THE CASTLE

Squeaking,
A black bat fluttering about in the dark dungeon.

Creaking,
A sneaky robber stepped clumsily on a loose floorboard.

Squawking,
The king's colourful parrot flapping noisily.

Talking,
The sad prisoners planning to escape quietly.

Singing,
The beautiful maid humming a lovely tune.

Ringing,
The loud servant bell calling the poor servant.

Laura Burgess (9)
Ashley CE Primary School

IN THE CASTLE

Scattering,
The autumn leaves lying on the ground outside.

Muttering,
The guards at the castle gates.

Squeaking,
A timid mouse was eating crumbs, under the dark table.

Creaking,
The brave knights were drawing in the heavy drawbridge.

Taunting,
The small children making fun of each other.

Haunting,
A ghost swooping in the castle.

Cheri Schoeman (9)
Ashley CE Primary School

THE CASTLE

Creaking,
A brave knight steps on an unnoticeable floorboard in the
                                        pitch-black dungeon.
Squeaking,
A small white rat goes into his big black hole.
Talking,
Guards whispering plans to attack the evil enemy.
Walking,
A knight strides along a dark thin corridor.
Taunting,
The wizard summoned a ghost out of a cauldron.
Haunting,
The ghost curses the wizard.

Mark Jackson (9)
Ashley CE Primary School

THE CASTLE

Crashing,
Dark bedroom windows fiercely blowing in the dreadful storm.

Smashing,
The clumsy bent butler dropping all the plates on the old wooden floor
In the kitchen.

Crying,
A little tiny baby fox squeaking outside, he's lost his mother.

Dying,
Prisoners sighing in the dark gloomy dungeons.

Talking,
Lots of groups of ghosts chatting in the long thin corridors.

Walking,
The old bent butler creeping down the old steep stairs.

Hayley Cobb (9)
Ashley CE Primary School

IN THE CASTLE

Creaking,
The clumsy maid steps on a floorboard in the dark spooky room.

Squeaking,
A small mouse is peeking through a crack in the wall.

Bashing,
A poltergeist dropping a pan on the kitchen floor.

Slamming,
In the dark room a brave knight bangs the door shut quickly.

Ringing,
An ugly stranger pushing a small doorbell.

Hissing,
A colourful snake slithering quietly under a creaky floorboard.

Emma Marsh (8)
Ashley CE Primary School

THE CASTLE

Dying,
The grumpy guard sitting by the old creaking door.
Crying,
A fierce ugly wolf outside the old door.

Crashing,
The windows hitting each other like never before.
Smashing,
The old white cutlery in the wind.

Dooming,
The castle in the haunted scary forest.
Booming,
The music in the top dark room.

Creaking,
The footsteps of a bent zombie.
Squeaking,
Bats flying fiercely overhead.

James Gray (10)
Ashley CE Primary School

THE HAUNTED CASTLE

Creaking,
The butler walking on the old battered floorboards.
Sneaking,
The naughty little ghost in the dark bedroom breaking toys
and precious antiques.
Weeping,
A little boy in the corner of the haunted bedroom.
Creeping,
A tall butler in the boy's bedroom stealing money.
Screaming,
A little girl under the dark gloomy floorboards suffocating
until she dies.

Beaming,
The fat ghost shouting and screaming while swinging.
Bashing,
A happy boy with his toys in his big red bedroom.
Crashing,
A good ghost hitting the nasty butler.

Lauren Jones (8)
Ashley CE Primary School

THE CASTLE

Creaking,
The dull floorboards outside the dark gloomy room.
Squeaking,
The old broken door wobbling in the misty eerie wind.

Snoring,
The sound of mice under a chair asleep and the king on the royal bed.
Pouring,
The rain tumbling down outside.

Grumbling,
The king's empty, hungry stomach.
Crumbling,
The ancient bricks on the grey wall dropping out onto the floor.

Abbie Key (9)
Ashley CE Primary School

THE CASTLE

Dripping,
Mysterious blood trickling down the spine of the bath
In the smoky toiletry room.
Ripping,
Green skin like mad in the dark, gloomy, cold basement.

Dying,
The sad, cold girl on the misty bed in the highest room.
Crying,
The weary vampire who lost its white bloody fangs
In the grubby bedroom.

Sneaking,
A shabby ghost in the smelly laundry taking out the raggy clothes
In the dark cellar.
Creaking,
Old floorboards rocking to and fro in the foggy ballroom.

Smashing,
A bent butler throwing thick glass in the backyard.
Crashing,
Round plates in the kitchen out of the gloomy cupboard
Which had lost its screws.

Jodie Dettloff (9)
Ashley CE Primary School

THE CASTLE

Haunting,
A ghost was circling the castle at night.

Screaming,
The queen has seen the ghost.

Hissing,
The sly snake bit the king's pinkie finger.

Kissing,
The queen made the king's pinkie finger better.

Taunting,
The king after beating the little dirty slave at cards.

Dreaming,
It's midnight and the maid is fast asleep.

Chris Sloan (9)
Ashley CE Primary School

THE CASTLE

Creaking . . .
The dusty cobwebbed doors swinging slowly open in the dim light.
Shrieking . . .
The long lost memories of the castle and the people gone forever.

Dripping . . .
The wearing, leaking pipe close to breaking.
Tripping . . .
The innocent falling lives, going, going, going gone.

Crying . . .
The awful sound of death, people never found again.
Dying . . .
The gloomy lost world of the ones you loved.

Smashing . . .
The high draughty window upstairs.
Crashing . . .
Precious china falling towards the rotting floor,
Like the lives from the curse.

Rosie Foster (10)
Ashley CE Primary School

SPOOKY CASTLE

Burning,
The flames of a fire crackle fiercely in the silent corridor,
Crackle! Crackle!

Churning,
The lady's tummy whirling round then a sudden scream
Ah she got beheaded.
Ah! Ah!

Creaking,
The king out of bed getting a drink, the guard stops him, the glass falls,
Smash! Smash!

Hissing,
The snake sliding slowly in the castle.
Hiss! Hiss!

Slapping,
The girl being hit very hard by a strong guard,
Slap! Slap!

Sophie Collins (9)
Ashley CE Primary School

IN THE CASTLE

Squeaking,
A cat magically turned into a fierce black rat.

Creaking,
The door noisily being opened by a ghost.

Crunching,
Someone tasting the burnt dinner.

Scrunching,
A hunter coming in with leaves stuck on his shoes.

Rattling,
A big scary skeleton has come to life.

Battling,
Oh no, the king is having a battle again but I think he's winning.
Hooray!

Rebecca Lee (8)
Ashley CE Primary School

THE CASTLE

Creaking,
The creaking floorboards in the tall spooky tower.
Squeaking,
An army of filthy smelly rats in the dark damp cellar.

Grumbling,
The old tired butler walking down the long dirty corridor.
Crumbling,
The staircase leading to the tall dark tower.

Crashing,
The rattling wooden drawbridge falling to the ground.
Smashing,
The shining silver cutlery being dropped by the old crooked maid.

Groaning,
The maid as she bends down to pick it up.
Moaning,
The ancient ghosts in the cold dark dungeon.

Andrew West (9)
Ashley CE Primary School

THE CASTLE

Screaming,
The guard was screaming in horror in the moat.

Dreaming,
The other guard was dreaming of dinner.

Hissing,
The bats hissing echoed in the dirty dungeon.

Missing,
But the bat missed his cave.

Dying,
The cook is suffocating in the tiny kitchen.

Crying,
The cook was screaming from pain.

Singing,
The joker has an awful song.

Ringing,
The joker was playing a song while the phone rang.

Andrew Gunner (10)
Ashley CE Primary School

SOUNDS OF A SPOOKY CASTLE

Singing,
The beautiful ladies dancing with the brave lords at a great ball.

Ringing,
The huge clock bells chime for midnight.

Muttering,
The royal guards chatting loudly about what goes on in the castle.

Stuttering,
The scared king carefully asking the wonderful queen to dance.

Slashing,
The horrid guards whipping a weak prisoner.

Crashing,
Plates being dropped on the kitchen floor.

Dying,
A clever rival roughly being conquered.

Sighing,
The mighty prince slowly sat down with relief.

Taunting,
The pretty queen in a rage because of the king's party.

Haunting,
Fearless ghosts creeping through the castle whispering terrible death.

Jade Benson (9)
Ashley CE Primary School

THE CASTLE

Crashing,
The massive stumble of an old bloody murdered housewife.
Smashing,
The massive bang of an old bent butler's room giving way.
Crying,
The angry wolf howling for his beautiful lost maid.
Dying,
The old muttered struggling prey of the angry wolf.
Moaning,
The old bent whimpering butler seeing his murdered housewife.
Leaping,
The camouflaged tiger jumping onto his prey.
Creeping,
The scary vampires searching silently for human flesh.
Creaking,
Fancy floorboards creaking badly in the tallest of towers.
Squeaking,
Hundreds of rats scurrying up the old stairs.
Dripping,
Gallons of blood dripping down from the top of the vampire's
sharp fangs.
Ripping,
Pointed vampire daggers feeding on people's blood and flesh.
Dreaming,
Crowds of people scared of the scary vampire's screaming
Thousands of people killed from the Black Death.

Nathan Toms
Ashley CE Primary School

THE CASTLE

Screaming,
A little boy running quickly from a spooky zombie.
Dying,
A person screeching from a spook with a short sword.
Creaking,
A mysterious door is opening in the courtyard.
Ringing,
A man is hitting a bell hard.
Slashing,
A man being beheaded badly.
Bashing,
A zombie knocking down the door.
Oh no!

Ryan Harvey (9)
Ashley CE Primary School

IN THE CREEPY CASTLE

Creaking,
A brave knight tiptoed past the king's bedroom.
Squeaking,
A small mouse running around looking for crumbs.
Slashing,
A long curtain getting caught on a pin sticking out.
Bashing,
A shiny sword falling slowly out of the brave knight's hands.

Collette Orton (9)
Ashley CE Primary School

THE CASTLE

Squeaking,
An oil black bat catching a grey mouse.
Creaking,
A manipulative murderer in the small attic.
Slashing,
A pearly ghost beheading a hunter.
Crashing,
A scared man running from the ghost fearfully.

Banging,
A troll banging a mini cannon.
Clanging,
The metal chains of a fearful hostage.
Dying,
A man after midnight in the deadly kitchen.
Crying,
A sad wife in a huddle over her husband.

Swooping,
A pale ghost on a running victim.
Whooping,
A ghost in killing celebration.
Haunting,
The emerald banshees in the dingy basement.
Taunting,
The black stone gargoyle by a pillar.

Talking,
The hostage going insane.
Walking,
The curious investigator by the hall.

Daniel Hall (10)
Ashley CE Primary School

THE CASTLE

Frightening,
Bats flew through the dining room quickly.

Lightening,
A flash outside in the unseen castle garden.

Sneaking,
A spider creeping round a shabby corner in a dark, dark loft.

Creaking,
An old man you cannot see but know is there.

Dripping,
Water from an ancient tap forgotten in a corner.

Ripping,
Rats nibbling quietly at a grubby shirt in a corner.

Bumping,
The gate creaking in the garden blowing in the wind.

Thumping,
A bent butler stumbles up the creaking stairs.

Crashing,
Plates falling out of a cupboard because a man opened it in the night.

Smashing,
Bats flew quickly through the grubby window of the highest room.

Dying,
A black rat sick of old age.

Crying,
An aged man shouting weakly in the cellar, cold and hungry,
Got locked there in the cold, years ago.

Jessica Lewsey (10)
Ashley CE Primary School

THE CASTLE

Moaning . . .
Frightening ghosts slowly going in and out of squeaky doors.
Groaning . . .
A strange looking figure going slowly into the cobwebby bedroom.
Rustling . . .
The ancient trees swaying in the blustery wind.
Bustling . . .
Old fashioned maids going into the bedroom with strange laundry.

Creaking . . .
Old black rats running on the collapsing floorboards.
Squeaking . . .
The old mouldy door blowing in the eerie wind.

Smashing . . .
Ghosts playing with the china plates in the leaky kitchen.
Crashing . . .
The almost blind butler walking into the massive bookshelf
That was covered in spider's cobwebs.

Dying . . .
The dumb horseman being severely executed.
Crying . . .
A miserable maid being harshly tortured by a very wicked witch.

Clattering . . .
A young knight in his shining armour heading towards
The spooky forest.
Pattering . . .
The ancient rusty tap dripping into the dusty sink.

Snoring . . .
An old unpleasant king in his chilly chambers.
Pouring . . .
Blood slowly trickling out of the headless horseman's neck.

Samantha Gray (9)
Ashley CE Primary School

THE FREAKY CASTLE

Smashing,
The windows were shattered and battered in the boomy, doomy room of
doom.
Crashing,
The ghostbusters hitting their car in dark park near the animal ark.
Bashing,
A green gruesome Frankenstein hitting his bolted head against the brick
wall in the freaky mass.

Richard Tickner (9)
Ashley CE Primary School

THE MINOTAUR

I am the Minotaur, alone in the dark,
Never to see the light of day,
Never to roam on the lush green grass,
Never to see the sun.
Just to feel on my hairy body
The slime and blood dripping off of me.
Pushing the bones on the floor,
My sharp horns like metal.
I am scared that a human might kill me.
I hear footsteps getting closer,
Louder, louder, louder.
What am I doing killing people who are not guilty?
I should be chewing the flesh of my master
And crunching his bones.
Then someone comes round the corner,
Draws his sword.
With one slash I fall,
Fall, fall, fall, fall, down to the ground.

Georgina Hewett (9)
Bramley School

SPACE

On Monday I went to space
But I didn't see much,
An alien flew into my face!

On Tuesday I went to Mars
A lovely place,
But a bit far.

On Wednesday I travelled to the sun
A tiny bit hot,
And not much fun.

On Thursday I went to Saturn
Quite interesting
And lots of things to learn.

On Friday I stayed right here
My favourite place,
That seems to be the best idea!

Katie Caddick (9)
Bramley School

IN THE LABYRINTH

In the labyrinth
Is where you never want to go
The wall of slime dripping down my hand
Or is it blood?
I hear the roar of the Minotaur
Then he comes round the corner
I draw my sword
With one slash he falls
What have I done?

Hannah Patrick (8)
Bramley School

DON'T GO

Snow, snow please don't go
I like you very much
You're cold and frosty to touch.

It will make me cry
When the land is dry
I will have nothing to do, without you.

Snow, snow if you go
Come back soon
Sometime before June.

Harriet Hewett (10)
Bramley School

THE OCEAN

Early in the morning
When the sun starts to rise
The calm soft ocean,
Opens its eyes.
Then the wind blows,
And the ocean goes mad
The calm ocean goes,
And the mad ocean is glad.

Ruth Connick (10)
Bramley School

BARKING MAD

I have a little dog
I think he's barking mad
I would not say he's never good
But most of the time he's bad.

He likes to play and he likes to run
He likes to steal my toys
And when he has a rattly thing
He makes a lot of noise.

Aimee King (9)
Bramley School

THE SUN IS OUT

The sun is out
It's shining bright
Children are playing
It's a wonderful sight
The flowers are opening in the sun
The grass is lush and green
Fruit hangs from branches by the ton
What a lovely sight to be seen.

Camilla Barden (8)
Bramley School

MINOTAUR IN THE LABYRINTH

I have never seen the outside world
I have never felt the sun
I am very lonely in this maze
I never have any fun.

I want to run in the fields of green
I want to play with you,
But I am stuck here in this maze
And I have feelings too!

Susannah Fownes (9)
Bramley School

I HAVE TWO DOGS

I have two German shepherds
I take them for a run
And they like chasing rabbits
And having lots of fun.

I like to take them to the woods
They try to climb the trees
They see the naughty squirrels
But all they do is tease.

I like to take them to the downs
To see the horses race
I like to see my dogs run fast
But they cannot go that pace.

I like to take them to the beach
They run into the sea
And then they dig up all the sand
And make a mess of me.

I like to take them to the pond
And listen to the frogs
There's lots to hear and lots to see
Oh yes I love my dogs.

Madeleine Kuhler (9)
Bramley School

IF I HAD . . .

If I had a magic rubber,
I would rub out the sting of a wasp.
I would rub out the smell of dirty socks.
I would rub out the squeak of the board pen.
I would rub out my mum saying no to sweets.

If I had a magic pencil
I would draw sweets that last for a year.
I would draw my bed everywhere.
So when I feel tired I can jump in
I would draw a rainbow in the sky when I am sad.

Sophie Gribben (10)
Bramley School

WHY I'D HATE MY CAT TO DIE

When I chose my cat,
I had to pick which one to buy.
From the first moment I saw her,
I'd hate my cat to die.

When I brought her home,
She looked like a very pretty tabby,
She has a beautiful furry tail,
Even though she's a little flabby.

She likes sleeping on my sister's bed,
She likes me stroking her tiny head,
She stands by her bowl and meows,
When she has not been fed.

When we cuddle up on the sofa
She's so warm and cosy,
When I'm doing private things
She's very, very nosy!

She likes chasing butterflies,
Birds, mice and bees.
Sometimes I get scratched
On my knobbly little knees!

Olivia Naylor (10)
Bramley School

MEMORIES, MEMORIES, CHILDHOOD MEMORIES

Miaow of the cat,
Feel of Granny's hat,
Taste of ice cream,
Sound of Lucy's scream,
Feel of cat clawing,
Sound of Grandad snoring.

Brand new dress,
Give Mum a rest,
New shoes for Lucy,
Strawberries ripe and juicy,
Teddy in my bed,
Daddy in the shed!

Emily Owen (10)
Bramley School

GIRAFFE

Kind, wild,
Beautiful browser
He's covered with patchwork
His neck is like a tree swaying
From side to side
Gentle leaner
He eats the leaves all day long
Till he's full!

Charlotte Wearn & Stephanie Young (10)
Bramley School

THE NOISES AT NIGHT

Boom, boom, boom, crack
Went the radiator
I got out of bed
I heard it again,
Boom, boom, boom.

Mmm, mmm, mmm,
Went the boiler
I got out of bed
What could it be?
Mmm, mmm, mmm.

I think I heard the telly
My mummy and daddy were watching
It was mysterious
Because when I went down it wasn't on!

Bang, bang, bang,
Went my brother
In a mood,
Threw all his toys on the floor
Bang, bang, bang.

Shout, shout, shout,
Shouted my dad getting annoyed with my naughty brother
Shout, shout, shout.

Shh, shh, shh,
Said my mum to my brother be quiet!
Danniella's trying to go to sleep!

Danniella Schindler (8)
Bramley School

MEMORIES, MEMORIES

Memories, memories, childhood memories
The very first taste of olives
And the smell of the bakery
The pastry piled up high!
Memories, memories, childhood memories
The feel of wood, rough, rough wood,
The feel of cotton, the fluffy, comfy cotton.
Memories, memories, childhood memories
My first tooth came out!
The crying and pain!
And out came my shout!
Santa Claus, Santa Claus coming
Present upon present
Memories, memories, childhood memories.

Jenny Shanks (10)
Bramley School

THE MINOTAUR'S MAZE

The Minotaur, the Minotaur
Oh his raging roar.
The Minotaur, the Minotaur
Oh the scraping of his hooves on the stone floor.
Is he round this corner?
Oh the Minotaur
The Minotaur, the Minotaur
Will I ever get out of here?
Nobody knows, nobody cares
We're in the Minotaur's lair.

Charlotte Bloodworth (8)
Bramley School

NOISES AT NIGHT

When I go to bed,
I hear,
The front door crash!
The dishes smash,
Mummy in a dash.
The radiator creaking,
And Anna squeaking,
The boiler bubbling,
And Laura squabbling,
In her sleep.
Mummy and Daddy murmuring
And the animals stirring,
I wonder what's occurring.

Lucy Houlding (8)
Bramley School

THE MAD ZOO

I went to the zoo and I saw
One sad snake,
Two happy hippopotamuses,
Three angry alligators,
Four slippery seals,
Five dancing deer,
Six wiggly whales,
Seven tipsy tigers,
Eight bubbly bears,
Nine mumbling monkeys,
Ten droopy dolphins,
What a strange day at the zoo!

Amy Wildgoose (8)
Bramley School

PIED PIPER'S PROMISE

The piper promised us milk chocolate rivers
The tune sounded like birds singing
He said there would be talking animals
And millions of sweets and chocolate bars
There would be mint grass and beautiful castles
The music made me follow, then the door closed . . .

The piper promised us smelly cheese and rotten eggs
The tune sounded like squeaking, scratching and nibbling
He said there would be smelly sewers and dirty gutters
And mouldy meat, banana skins and gone-off milk
There would be fish bones, mouldy fruit and smelly dustbins
The music made me go after it, then we came to the river . . .

Laura McLean (10)
Bramley School

EXCUSES, EXCUSES

Well, first of all
A flying saucer landed on my lawn.
Then these little green men came out!
They said 'Take me to your homework,'
They put me in a kind of trance
And I couldn't control myself!
Before I knew it
I had given them my homework!
Then they chuckled an evil laugh
'Ha! Ha! Ha!'
But they did give me a puppy instead
And *that's* why I haven't got my homework.

Bethany Wardle (9)
Bramley School

JACK FROST

Jack Frost, Jack Frost,
You're here, you're here,
Don't go away,
I want to play!

You're making my garden,
Glisten like a pearl,
Don't worry, don't worry
I'm only a girl!

When I go out,
Please don't nip my toes,
Or bite my nose
When I run about!

Jack Frost, Jack Frost
Why do you go?
I want to play with you in the snow.

Rebecca Rainback & Alice Boulding (11)
Bramley School

EXCUSES, EXCUSES

Well Miss,
I had to go to the dentist,
The dentist pulled
All my teeth out,
When he wasn't supposed to pull out any
He gave me a filling
When I didn't need a drilling -

And *that's why* I'm late for school!

Clare Bushell (9)
Bramley School

MEMORY NUMBERS

I walked at one,
I talked at two,
And three and four and five.

Count down till Christmas
1, 2, 3,
I wonder what Santa's
Got for me.

I walked at one,
I talked at two,
And three and four and five.

I started school at three years old
And learnt to do what I was told.

I walked at one,
I talked at two,
And three and four and five.

Emily Howard (10)
Bramley School

DRUMS AND THUNDERBOLTS

Drums banging,
Thunderbolts crashing,
Scrapes of stones on the windows,
Volcanoes erupting,
Winds like cannons booming
Vicious crashing,
Rain like hurting spears
It's like a giant moving my house
The sea is lashing with madness.

Sarah Muggleton (9)
Bramley School

HIDE-AND-SEEK

'Ready or not, here I come' comes the voice,
I hope that this hiding place was a good choice.

I'm hiding in my bedroom 'cause we're playing hide-and-seek
Actually I bet you that the seeker had a peek!

I can smell the food that I'm having for my tea,
Mum's cooking my favourite meal just for me!

I can hear the seeker coming, I can hear her grumbling
I'm just hoping that my tummy won't start rumbling!

I can see a Kitkat wrapper, a vest and a sock,
I can hear the tick-tocking of my clock.

'Found you!' says a voice as I see the seeker's head,
Did you guess where I was hiding?
I was under my bed!

Katie Buckhalter (11)
Bramley School

EXCUSES, EXCUSES

Well, a spaceship
Landed in my garden
And an alien came in the house
And took us away
To Mars and back
I was holding my homework
When we took off
My work blew away into space!
And *that's* why I don't have my homework Miss!

Lauren Morton (9)
Bramley School

HIDE-AND-SEEK

Come and get me!
I am hiding in my bed
I can smell my pillowcase and sheets
I can't see anything in here
Something is coming
I go quieter
I stop breathing
Curl up tight
It came up onto my bed
Oh! It's my cat
Then I hear something else
It comes up onto my bed again
Oh! Again it's my sister's cat
My sister hears the cat
I hear my sister
She comes on my bed
And jumps on me!
She has found me!

Sophie Grice (10)
Bramley School

BABY BAT

Clinging on with teeth and toes
Seeing all the wintry snows
Swooping up and swooping down
Somersaulting all around.

Eating all the crispy moths
Skimming all the dying crops
Mother holds me tight all night
Never seeing a spot of light.

Nicola Taylor (9)
Bramley School

MEMORIES

When I walked for the first time one day
I let go of my mother's hand and took a step away.

It wasn't long before I learnt to run
The days went running by.

The baby food I had to eat,
The milk I had to drink.

The toys people used to buy for me
They're old and shabby now.

Decorating the Christmas tree
Putting the stars on the top
That was my favourite time of all.

Natasha Ward (11)
Bramley School

BATS

The night was black,
The moon was out,
The stars were wandering high.
The bats came out,
They screamed about
I heard their piercing cry.

They swooped and looped,
They soared above,
They spun around and round
In dark midnight,
They took their flight,
Woods echoed with their sound.

Susannah Long (9)
Bramley School

THE SNOW

The snow is falling,
Falling,
Falling.

The snow is calling,
Calling,
Calling me out to play.

Outside there's a new world
That no one has ever walked on
It's a piece of paper never been written on,
A sheet that's never been slept on.

The snow is falling,
Falling,
Falling.

The snow is calling,
Calling,
Calling me out to play.

Emily Eason (10)
Bramley School

STORMY NIGHTS

The wind is whistling and howling
The lightning is like threatening flames in the air
I feel like the world is going to end
I feel like bullets are going off everywhere
And guns are going off
With bangs and roars
The clouds are getting blacker and blacker
And the air is poisonous.

Sarah Phillips (10)
Bramley School

ANIMALS

I went to the zoo
With my friends like you
And saw,
Henry the horse
He's friendly of course!
Gerald Giraffe how he loves to laugh!
Not forgetting the sheep that bleats
Oh! All these animals are so very sweet.

Badgers and bats and
Cool, clever cats
They love to eat fat smelly rats!
Harold the hen coughs now and again
He's got a bad cold 'cause he's getting old
Ellie the elephant trumpets her way
Throughout the night and throughout the day.

Well that's the end of the great time!

Sydney White (9)
Broomfield House School

ROBINS AND RATS

Robins and rats,
Elephants and cats,
Handsome horses and dirty old bats,
Gerald giraffe oh how he loves to laugh and
Sarah the sheep she loves to bleet.
All these animals are very sweet
So what about a bird who loves to tweet
Or Elliot the eagle he's got the measles
Or David the dog.

Phoebe Small (8)
Broomfield House School

ROBINS TO RATS

The robin flew high in the air that day,
Not remembering about the bill he had to pay,
But suddenly what did he see over there
A small tiny creature with lots of grey hair,
He flew down but not too far,
Just in case it was a car.
The robin flew down a little further
Now thinking it was not a murderer,
He called down to the tiny creature,
'Hey young fellow you've got some ugly features.'
The robin flew down and down
And his red breast looked like a wonderful gown,
And after a while they made quite good friends
Robins and rats imagine that.

Charlotte Owen (9)
Broomfield House School

ROBINS TO RATS

The robin flies through the night,
Looking at everything
Light and bright
Head lamps to car lights and wild cats eyes
Then he flies back to the barn,
Where he sleeps all night.

Robin looked down and saw
Something running on the floor,
It made a noise, a terrible noise,
So Robin swooped down and picked Rat off the ground.

Francesca Miller (9)
Broomfield House School

BADGERS TO BATS

While the night is closing in
The badger collects his last tin,
The bat glides away
In the moonlight and
Finds his way into a silver bin,
Gets his win
Eats his din -
While gliding through the dark treetops.

The badger shines his large eyes,
The old brown owl cries
Twitt twoo! I see you!

The bat hears with his little ears
And flutters down to see what he can find.

Polly Kemp-King (8)
Broomfield House School

FOXES TO FOXGLOVES

Foxes are sly,
Like a hawk in the sky,
Foxgloves are pretty,
(Just like my kitty),
Fox cubs are playful
They'll knock down your table
Foxgloves look elegant,
Unlike an elephant,
So it's
Foxes to foxgloves for me
So you'll see.

Emma Robson (8)
Broomfield House School

FOXES TO FOXGLOVES

Said the fox to his wife
'I shall take strife to make you a flower garden,
But dear I don't see what you want for me to get for your
flower garden.'
She said,
'Roses and primroses, foxgloves and cats' toes
Why all of these would be quite fine
Come on now it is time to dine'
She gave a spring of foxgloves
To remember her by
She said
'Don't forget to brush your teeth'
As she said this he gave a sigh.
The roses and primroses all were quite fine,
The cats toes were really easy but the foxgloves were
Really quite problems so he hugged the foxgloves
His wife had given him and out fell a seed!
He returned to his wife who said 'Hooray
You're back, here is a surprise for you'
And in a cot was a little fox baby
With foxgloves on his fingers and toes.

Natalie York (9)
Broomfield House School

BADGERS TO BATS

Badgers to bats,
Monkeys and cats
They all wear very funny hats.
Dancing and prancing all day long,
They sing a very silly song.

Whenever you hear a gong,
You know they're singing their silly song
They're grooving and moving all night long,
And they're letting you feel the beat till dawn!

Kate Hare (9)
Broomfield House School

FOXES TO FOXGLOVES

A fox once on a winter's day
Had very cold paws and said, 'I say!
Oh, what a fox needs is a set of mittens,
And if I don't get some I'll say, oh kittens!'

So he padded into a shop and bought
The perfect set of gloves he thought
They were purple sheep's wool with flowers on
And he wore them all winter until the sun shone!

Rosalind Gealy (9)
Broomfield House School

BADGER TO BATS

Badgers and bats
Never hang with cats,
They never stick together
Because they like different weather
Some give a buzz others give a neigh.

A buzz or a
Bizz it doesn't matter which
But badgers and bats never hang with cats.

Alex Dass (8)
Broomfield House School

ROBINS TO RATS

Robins and rats,
Elephants to cats,
All wear silly looking hats.
Elephants are fat, cats look like rats
Mother cats play in their baths.

Robins and rats,
Elephants to cats,
All wear silly looking hats.

My robin looks like Mr Cat but
Mr Cat eats my rats.
My father looks like a big rat
Only when he says 'Rat'!

Robins and rats,
Elephants to cats,
All wear silly looking hats.

Oliver Burman (8)
Broomfield House School

BADGERS AND BATS

Badgers and bats,
Never eat cats.
But the cat always like to eat rats.

Cats and doggies,
Pigs and hoggies,
Doggies are hiding behind big loggies.

Cats hate baths,
And the hyenas laugh,
But don't forget badgers and bats!

Oliver Turner (8)
Broomfield House School

MACBETH ON THE BLASTED HEATH

The clouds overcast the heath,
The rain down-poured like rocks smashing my face,
The jet black trees creaked and looked like clutching fingers,
The swamp, murky and army green coloured,
The grass was turning scarlet,
Clouds orange,
Emerald eyes appeared.

The ravens screeching,
The devil's dog snarling,
The wind was howling like wolves,
The immoral sounds of dead soldiers,
The mighty sounds of swords claiming,
The screaming of innocent people dying,
The rocks started to speak to me.

I was seeing children, then turning spirals,
I saw as I was walking, dead rats stained with blood,
The trees making shapes of twisted witches necks,
Suddenly in the distance I saw a cauldron and the three crooked
witches,
Double, double toil and trouble,
Fire burn and cauldron bubble,

My eyes eternally froze
Witches grouped
Cauldron exploded.

Sam Colgate (11)
Byfleet Primary School

MACBETH

The clouds were looming
Across the grey shadowy sky.
Wind whirling and shattering
The dry, crusty leaves blowing them high.
The tall crooked trees
Edging towards the dark, damp castle.
In the misty distance of the glowing moonlight.

Macbeth strolled across the stony marsh
Noticing the wide piercing eyes
Glaring at him,
Through the green rustling bushes
Rain lashing down
Deafening thunder striking.
All there was to be heard in the distance
Was the cackle of witches laughing,
The potion being stirred
And the bubbles dripping
Over the side of the black witches' cauldron.

Megan Parry (10)
Byfleet Primary School

MACBETH ON THE BLASTED HEATH

The thick black trees were swaying frantically
Lashing rain stinging my face like a swarm of bees
Fog falling like a blanket on my face
Blinding flash of lightning lit up the sky.

Barking dogs galloped past with madness in their eyes!
Wind was heavy blowing the trees
Someone screaming in fear or in pain
Evil howls coming from trees.

There were bent shapes of three women
The trees branches were banging my face
The owls were looking down at me
The black figures were dancing around a big round pot
The wind was whirling like a wild hurricane and
Whirled away.

Kimberley Oxborough (10)
Byfleet Primary School

MACBETH ON THE BLASTED HEATH

On the blasted heath trees were dancing
Marshes are muddy
Clouds creeping over Scotland
Squelching in the marsh and slipping everywhere
The unlit sky dark and gloomy
After battle.

The wind howling violently is like a dog
Voices echoing against the trees
Thunder crashing louder than ever
Inky black rats running past noisily
Dogs howling restlessly and
Hags cackling.

Movement appears too quick for a blind eye
Jet-black silhouettes moving
A shine catches his eye
A bony finger points
What's going on here?
Something's brewing.

Lucy O'Leary (10)
Byfleet Primary School

ON TOP OF THE BLASTED HEATH

On top of the blasted heath
Trees creeping and dancing in a circle,
Rocks sinking into the boggy marshland.
Clouds casting overhead,
Rain pouring
Marshland expanding.
Thunder bellowing like a mighty king's laugh.
Wind howling like a dog in pain,
Witches screaming and chanting
Leaves rustling in the wind.
Wind whistling,
Cauldron bubbling.
Witches throwing in toads and frogs,
Lightning shocking and sparking.
The witches grabbing my legs and urging me along the marshland.
Walking into danger
And the unknown.

Stephen Braine (11)
Byfleet Primary School

MACBETH ON THE BLASTED HEATH

The castle dark and deadly
The trees swishing and swaying in the distance
The clouds getting darker, darker, darker
Sky starless
Castle still.

'Double, double toil and trouble'
You could hear from the castle walls
Owls hooting, wolves howling
Witches laughing, laughing, laughing
Wind whistling,
Witches watching.

Figures rustling among the golden leaves
Branches grasping,
Eyes in the tops of trees,
Watching over shadows looming, looming, looming.

Melissa Warner (11)
Byfleet Primary School

MACBETH ON THE BLASTED HEATH

Trees probing like a dead man's fingers
Ravens plucking at a rotting carcass
Clouds lurking in the dismal trees
The barren marsh hidden in the inky darkness
Figures waiting,
Eyes watching.

The thunder was booming out above the soundless night
The howling wind whistling past the jagged rocks
Ravens calling over the dark dreary heath
The leafless trees creaking in the squall
Feet moving,
No turning.

Silhouettes stealthily moving across the desolate heath
Torn robes flapping in the draconian wind
Figures shrouded in mystery waiting to be found
Shapes twirling in the darkness
Chanting, chanting,
Chanting.

Sam Royston (10)
Byfleet Primary School

MACBETH ON THE BLASTED HEATH

The rain bursting out of the sky,
The witches cluttered together making howling noises,
I see evil above the clouds,
I'm having scary dreams,
Trees swaying and screaming,
The fog camouflaging me,
The sky drifting and the thunder clapping
As loud as it possibly can.

The sounds are making terrible noises,
The branches are alive,
Squelching noises are made with the leaves,
Everything is misty grey,
The wind is stabbing me as hard as it can,

Faces grinning,
Everything has faded,
Faded, faded, gone.

Lauren White (11)
Byfleet Primary School

MACBETH ON THE BLASTED HEATH

On top of the blasted heath,
Trees bare arms are bent,
The marshes steadfast,
Rocks' crooked edges covered in slime,
Marsh boggy,
Witches crooked.

The last leaves on the trees whistling,
Creatures calling and shuddering,
Witches dropping charms in the cauldron
Thunder as fierce as a tiger when hungry,
Witches stirring,
Creatures calling.

Witches silhouette in the mist,
Lightning like a twig,
Outlines the crooked witches,
Creatures howling, birds chanting, witches dancing,
Macbeth's destiny,
Looming over him.

Alex Doune (11)
Byfleet Primary School

ON BLASTED HEATH

On blasted heath at dead of night,
Clouds are looming,
Bushes are whispering,
Faster, faster through the dark,
Treacherous marshes hold me back,
I'm riding, riding through the dark!

On blasted heath at dead of night,
A raven called, an owl shrieks,
Creaking trees that bar my way,
Bats a-hunting call me thither,
The howling wind a calls me thither,
I'm riding, riding through the dark!

On blasted heath at dead of night,
To my eye a fire light flickers,
Lightning flicks above my head,
Silhouetted shapes are calling me,
Macbeth, Macbeth,
I'm riding, riding through the dark!

Caitlin Powell (11)
Byfleet Primary School

MACBETH ON TOP OF THE BLASTED HEATH

Clouds covering the last bit of sky,
The muddy swamp bubbling,
Birds swooping down to collect the last dead rat
The trees all bent down crouching like little old men,
Using branches for walking sticks
The trees bending, bending down to the ground, ground, ground.
On top of the blasted heath you can hear and see it all,
The swamp bubbling, bubbling, bubbling,
The last leaf falling, falling,
The wind shouting with anger.
While rushing past the faces of innocent men,
Pushing and pulling them down to the ground, ground, ground.
At last he finds the witches
He walks but does not seem to be going anywhere.
In his sight he can see the bellowing of the trees,
And the cauldron red hot while spitting in his face.
The thunder roaring with madness,
And the lightning slashing the trees with its fire.
As the three witches watch the trees fall to the ground, ground.

Daniel Axten-Jones (10)
Byfleet Primary School

MACBETH ON THE BLASTED HEATH

Dead trees probing like old men's fingers
Crows plucking at the rotting carcass
Dark clouds prowling in the dismal trees
The bleak barren marshes hidden in the inky darkness
    Figures waiting
    Silhouettes moving.

Trees howling in the milky moonlit sky
Echoing giggles screeching in the eerie silence
Fearsome lightning, striking the withered branches
Hair-raising crashes of bellowing thunder
    Sinister sounds
    Looming noises.

Dark shadows furtively swirling in the distance
Fabric-shrouded figures swaying in unison
Jagged shapes moaning . . . muttering
Three malicious witches sneering repeatedly
    Cauldron bubbling
    Fire crackling . . .

Matthew Ogbourn (11)
Byfleet Primary School

MACBETH ON THE BLASTED HEATH

Above the marsh,
Creeping rocks
Tearing reeds, foggy clouds
Craggy ripples,
The dark dullness of the wind
Blowing the bare leaves
Haunting the night
Crackling chants.

The sight of Macbeth
Twirling in a twinkle
Squelching through the dirt
Roaring shadows
Ranging reeds.

Haunting howls
Rippled sounds
Stretching black
Lacy coils
Urging fog
Flurry log
Still as a statue
Macbeth stood
Alone in the wood.

Tia Render (10)
Byfleet Primary School

It Was So Quiet . . .

It was so inaudible you could hear the wave brushing on the sand
                              on a hot summer's day.
It was so peaceful that you could hear the rain falling in the sky
                              whilst walking down the street.
It was so muted that you could hear a page being turned in a book
                              on a table or dream.
It was so dead that you could hear people rising from the grave
                              on a cold autumn's night.
It was so hushed that you could hear a leaf fall from a tree
                              on a winter's day.
It was so soundless that you could hear a seed growing
                              into the great oak.
It was so speedless that everyone was miming and only the mice
                      and small delicate things could be heard.

Luca Sepe (11)
Cuddington Community Primary School

Take Two

The sun snores soothingly,
The chimney pots rock back and forward,
A wisp of snow twirls around,
Streaks of lightning scar the black,
A ferocious colony of hail thuds down,
A fury of mist dashes around,
A sleek quilt of frost blankets the ground.

Pierre Timms (9)
Cuddington Community Primary School

QUIETNESS

It was so quiet I could hear a hummingbird flapping its wings
                        in the silent sky.
It was so inaudible I could hear Claude Monet's brush
                        sailing across the thin white paper.
It was so serene I could hear William Shakespeare
                        scratching the white paper with his fine inked feather.
It was so muted I could hear the water droplets gathering
                        in the morning rain clouds.
It was so peaceful I could hear the wind howling through
                        the thick green forest.
It was so placid I could hear a pin falling downwards
                        soaring through the air.
It was so calm I could hear a fish darting through the sea
                        like a silver arrow.
It was so noiseless I could hear an egg hatch and a baby bird
                        taking its first peep at the world.

Jievagan Bala (11)
Cuddington Community Primary School

THE GO-KART

I step into the go-kart it is sleek and elegant like a bird
                        riding the sky.
The engine starts, it is a lion roaring after devouring its crippled prey.
The kart rolls onto the scorched tarmac, it's a snake crawling towards
                        an unknown enemy.
I boot the engine, I am a cheetah chasing his meal.
I turn sharply, it is a sleek whip cracking through the cool midnight air.
Another kart bashes me, it's a hammer striking home.
I cross the line to many cheers, the predator has won once more.

Daniel Mills (11)
Cuddington Community Primary School

THE ROLLER COASTER

The speeding boat glides along the metal river,
Swooshy, swish, swooshy, swish,
Boarding passengers pull down their safety harnesses,
Clack, clack, clack, clack,
The motor is operated, it zims along,
Clackety, clack, clackety, clack.
The waterfall approaches, everyone screams,
They are precipitation, falling down the current tide
They are the birds gliding into the mist below
They are the river returning to the sea
The river calms, the passengers unload
They are the boats, returning to dock for the long day ahead.

Lauren Marks (11)
Cuddington Community Primary School

IT WAS SO QUIET . . .

It was so tranquil I could hear the pitter, patter of a deer.
It was so placid I could hear the soaring waves of ocean clear.
It was so serene I could hear the sad emotion of fear.
It was so soundless I could hear the falling thud of someone's tear.
It was muted I could hear the days and months of one whole year.
It was so peaceful I could hear the sound and echoes in someone's ear.
It was so calm I could hear the bubble and fizz of an open beer.
It was so silent I could hear the hustle and bustle of a tourist pier.
It was so noiseless I could hear the moans and groans of someone
queer.
It was so hushed I could hear the breathing movement of someone near.

Hayley Copland (11)
Cuddington Community Primary School

THE MAGIC BOX

I will put in the box . . .
The curving colours of a cosy curtain on a candlelit night,
Inferno from the nostrils of an angry father,
The sound of sight seeing a shriek.

I will put in the box . . .
A cat with a throbbing stomach,
A gulp of the clearest water from the River Nile,
A bounding flash from a terminal fish.

I will put in the box . . .
Five coloured wishes spoken in Spanish,
The latest joke from an early friend,
And the first beam of a baby.

I will put in the box . . .
A thirteenth month and an orange moon,
A table outside in a field,
And a tree growing inside a room.

My box is fashioned from mercury and nickel and pewter,
With planets on the lid and love in the corners,
Its hinges are everybody's shoulder joints clicking in.

I shall ski in my box
From the top of Mount Everest,
Then go up a ramp and end up at home
When I realise time started again . . .

Michael Niven (9)
Cuddington Community Primary School

THE MAGIC BOX

I will put in the box . . .
The calming colours of a curtain on a candle lit night,
The inferno of an angry dad,
The whirling hair touching my white head.

I will put in the box . . .
A pot of coal wrenched from a fire,
A drink from the darkest ocean,
A delicate swift flashing from a tropical fish.

I will put in the box . . .
Five bright talent mixed in a bowl,
The sight of a blind man,
The last smile of a king.

I will put in the box . . .
A first cheer and a last song,
A wizard in a coffin,
And a mummy in a haunted house.

My box is old but still in use
With corners full of joy,
Its lid shouting to be opened
But scared to be closed.

I will dance in my box
On the twisty turning slide
Then dive in water in a glittering tide.

Hayley Randall (10)
Cuddington Community Primary School

THE MAGIC BOX

I will put in the box . . .
The warm colours of a Chinese curtain,
The flames from the nostrils of a livid father,
The smell of summer air swishing and swaying.

I will put in the box . . .
A book quivering,
The water from a magical waterfall,
The tropical fish never seen before.

I will put in the box . . .
One special wish spoken in a language unknown,
The will from the very first king,
And the birth of a beautiful princess.

I will put in the box . . .
A friendly land and a glowing moon,
A star drinking water,
And a ghost riding a camel.

My box is fashioned from crystals and rubies,
With magic stars on the lid and whispers in the corners,
Its hinges are gold
Like a one pound coin.

I shall sail in my box,
On the calm seas in sunlight,
Then wash ashore on a country in the desert,
The colour of a shiny rainbow.

Chloe Bissell (10)
Cuddington Community Primary School

THE MAGIC BOX

I will put in my box . . .
A washing line wedged with washing swaying in the wind,
The roar of a Ferrari coming to a stop,
A tarantula thought to travel to Tenerife.

I will put in my box . . .
A stiff lady with pins and needles in her leg,
A crunch from some crackling on a Sunday roast,
A soaring glide from a starving golden eagle.

I will put in the box . . .
A final warning murmured in a speech,
The first ever word from a baby sister,
The last ever smile from a great, great grandad.

I will put in the box . . .
A tenth planet discovered in 2001,
A grown-up playing at nursery,
A baby poking its tiny fingers into computer keys.

My box is full with glory
Rubies, crystals, diamonds and gems,
And miles of fantastic memories,
And transparent, delicate and fragile glass.

I will change things in my box
Like make my home on a tropical island
Or make a millennium each year
So far from the dazzling sun.

William Chipperton (9)
Cuddington Community Primary School

IT WAS SO QUIET . . .

It was so placid I could hear the stars twinkling beside the yellow
moon at the strike of midnight.

It was so dead I could hear the clouds moving loitering like a snail
on a pale blue piece of paper.

It was so still that I could hear a lonely caterpillar eating a timid leaf
until it was obsolete.

It was so silent you could hear the characters talking in the imaginary
pages of a book disturbingly at bedtime stories.

It was so hushed you could hear the gleaming of a magical rainbow
glittering once the rain had gone.

It was so calm you could hear the rain in the clouds forming doubling
and cloning and multiplying quickly once evaporated.

It was so noiseless you could hear the cries of a fly, trapped in a
Spider's web, ready to be drained and gone forever at the break of day.

It was so quiet you could hear the wick burning on a candle rapidly
once lit and going to be gone forever.

It was so quiet you could hear the chisel on a sculpture chipping itself,
being hit by the overworked sculptor, at the crack of dawn.

It was so silent I could hear the slow ticking of a clock into
the new millennium.
Suddenly, it wasn't silent anymore.

Rebecca Dear (10)
Cuddington Community Primary School

IT WAS SO QUIET . . .

It was so undetectable I could hear a pencil being sharpened under
A splintered wooden desk just as we are dismissed for an early lunch.

It was so silent I could hear a bird's wing flapping as it let out
                                                    a gust in the sunrise.

It was so placid I could hear the tapping of a typewriter
                                                    in an old mansion.

It was so still I could hear the turn of a holy page in a bible
                                                    at an evening ceremony.

I was so calm I could hear a pond skater swimming across a pond
                                                    surface in a local park.

It was so muted I could hear the swish of a paintbrush on a sea
                                                    of white paper.

It was so peaceful I could hear a scuttling termite eating away
                                                    at the rotten floorboards.

It was so inaudible I could hear a morning wake up call from a rooster
                                                    at the nearby farm.

It was so soundless I could hear the monstrous waves crushing against
                                                    the helpless sand.

It was so quiet I could hear ink rushing from my pen as it touches
                                                    the fine paper.

Perry O'Neill (11)
Cuddington Community Primary School

IT WAS SO QUIET

It was so placid I could hear the flap of a wary bird's wing searching
for its wiggling prey.

It was so still I could hear the swaying of a whispering tree waving
at me in the moonlight.

It was so hushed I could hear the screaming of a plant begging for
refreshing water burning in the heat of the scorching sun.

It was so muted I could hear the waking of a decaying corpse pleading
for its lost life.

It was so soundless I could hear electricity bursting down the wires with
a buzz of a bee turning on the lamp as I settle into my book.

It was so calm I could hear the voice of an angel calling unwanted souls
sending a message from God as I settle into the holy book.

It was so quiet I could hear the howl of a wolf howling at the ball of
cheese in the sky whilst I drift off to dreamland.

It was so silent I could hear the snore of a distant dreamer dreaming of
peace on Earth as I drift further into dreamland.

It was so quiet I could hear no sound except for the gentle thumping of
my heart as I lay in my bed with the warmth of the blazing fire.

Catherine Fyson (11)
Cuddington Community Primary School

SEASONS

In spring I like to
See the flowers growing
Through the ground.

In summer they are
Colourful and bright
Standing in the sun.

In autumn the bushes,
Shrubs and trees are bare
Leaves on the ground.

In winter it's cold
The plants are asleep
Waiting for spring
So they can begin to peep.

Amy Robinson (9)
Doods Brow School

I HAD NO FRIENDS

I had no friends at all
Until you came my way
And now we play and play all day
I only hope you never
Have to go away
It would be sad
To lose the only friend
I ever really had.

Danielle Smith (10)
Doods Brow School

MY BED

I woke up in my bed this morning,
Long before the day was dawning.
I snuggled down and tried to sleep,
Then I took a little peep.
At first I thought that there was someone at the door.
Then I noticed it was clothes on the floor.
Oh what an untidy boy I am,
Not as bad as my brother Sam.

I looked again just to check,
Then I began to strain my neck.
I lent back down,
Then I found the cat on my bed,
She was meowing because she hadn't been fed.
I took her down and went back up.
I went to sleep without a peep
But when I woke up I was still half asleep.

Andrew Dorgan (10)
Doods Brow School

HOLIDAY

I'm going on my holiday
And I'm staying there forever.
I'm going on my holiday
Where there's some sunny weather.

I'm going on my holiday
Where the sun is shining.
I'm going on my holiday
Where there's a silver lining.

I'm going on my holiday
Lots of postcards I'll have to send.
I'm going on my holiday
And I can't bring a friend.

I'm going on my holiday
I wish you could come too.
I'm going on my holiday
Goodbye, taraa, talloo.

Sophie Harrison (9)
Doods Brow School

MY TIME MACHINE

I woke up in the morning, went downstairs
There was my time machine
I just remembered I'd had my clothes on for five days but never mind
I got into my time machine, I closed the door
I pulled the handle and then I was off
In two seconds I was in the 1940s
There was a war
So I pulled the handle
Then I was in the time of the Tudors
It was smelly
Then I pulled the handle again
I was with the dinosaurs
So I got a stick and took off my clothes
And waved it at the dinosaurs
And the dinosaurs went away
So I put the time to 2001 and went home.

Craig Lawrence (10)
Doods Brow School

EARTHQUAKE IN INDIA

The steady shake of the rock-hard earth
Startled the people of South Asia.
Maybe it's the time when one is coming to birth
Its scared mother would run round India.

The shaking started at eight o'clock
And shook out for miles around.
The severe jog shook every rock,
There was a dreadful sound.

The forty-five seconds were frightening,
Until the blast-off came.
It struck the people like lightning,
And it was terrible all the same.

It knocked the buildings down like matchsticks
And shattered them to bits on the floor.
Rocks stung the people like javelin sticks,
And down on them came more.

Then everything was ruined,
And most of the people were covered.
And down on the floor they were pinned,
But suddenly, over them, a silence hovered.

No one knew what happened,
Some were worried about daughter and son.
Then they realised, even the people down pinned,
The earthquake. It was over and done.

Footnote

The police are still searching.
Some lost hope, some didn't.
Some people are dead, some are alive.
Some are unknown and haven't been found yet.
Some are buried by rocks or by sad people.
Sirens are screaming and vehicles bringing people to places.
But for the rest, let us wish them hope and good luck.

Ali Jawad (10)
Doods Brow School

RABBITS

Rabbits are cuddly, rabbits are sweet
I love the way they stand up on two feet.

Rabbits are jumpy, they like to hop
They run about and then they just flop.

Rabbits eat vegetables, they love to munch
They like lots of lettuce and carrots to crunch.

Rabbits have pointy ears and bright eyes
I love it when they look up to the skies.

Rabbits have whiskers and noses that twitch
It's as though they have a constant itch.

Rabbits are black, brown and white
They are mostly friendly but sometimes they bite.

Rabbits are fun, they make me giggle
They jump up in the air and then they jiggle.

I like ones with stripes, I like ones with spots
Whatever they look like, I love rabbits lots.

Jack Hayes (8)
Doods Brow School

MY ADVENTURE

There's a monster in my house
It wants to come and eat me!
It doesn't think I'm small and thin
It thinks I'm big and meaty!

I know what I'll do
I'll have to go and hide.
There's a cupboard in my room,
So I think I'll get inside.

Suddenly I'm in Sweetie Land
With sweets and sweets galore.
I'm standing on a marzipan path,
Nearby's a house with an open door.

Suddenly out of the door,
Comes an old and ugly witch.
She grabs me by my sleeve,
And throws me in a ditch!

But the ditch has no bottom,
I'm falling and falling
And then I'm in my room,
And my mum is calling.

'Eleanor what's the matter with you?
Why didn't you come and see?
Why, I've been calling for ages,
Now, you must come down for tea!'

Eleanor Bolus (10)
Doods Brow School

THE MAGIC MAN

I was walking to my house,
On a summer's day.
And on the way,
I saw a man sitting on a sleigh.

His name was Maverick,
And he said he was magic.
But I know magic doesn't exist.

I told him he's a fake,
So he said to me,
I'd be scratched by a rake.

Then something fell from the sky,
And then it scratched me on the thigh,
I saw it was a rake,
After all he's not fake.

I told him I was sorry,
And he made me load his lorry.
And I'll never do this again
He gave me a lolly,
For loading the lorry.

Then I went home,
And never saw him again.

Anish Majmudar (10)
Doods Brow School

FOUR SEASONS

We wrap up warm in winter clothes,
And often get a runny nose.
Snowflakes falling from the sky,
Floating down from way up high.
The snow is great to play in,
I love to go tobogganing.
Spring is here hip, hip hooray!
It's nearer to a summer's day.
Blossom appears upon the trees,
Ready for the buzzy bees.
Woolly lambs are born once more,
With such cute faces I adore.
If you get up at the crack of dawn,
You'll see wild baby rabbits upon your lawn.
Summer time is really great!
It reminds me of Doods Brow School fête.
Summer holidays are such good fun
With buckets and spades,
And lots of sun.
I'm feeling hot,
I need to cool down,
I have to find a shady spot.
Autumn leaves are falling down,
Tossing and turning all around.
Shades of red and golden brown,
Make a carpet on the ground.
It's getting cold let's wrap up warm
Ready for a winter's storm
I can't believe a year has passed,
The seasons just go by so fast.

Sophia Cardillo (10)
Doods Brow School

JOURNEY TO URANUS

The journey starts in Florida, USA,
The shuttle takes off at ten today,
We roar up into the air,
We're going into space.

We zoom past magnificent, magical Mars,
Strapped down so we don't float off
Onto maroon Mars.

On we go past jazzy, jovial Jupiter,
Keeping our distance so we're not sucked in,
Into the orange jam, Jupiter.

We fly past super Saturn,
We've now been going for a very long time,
Through the dark reaches of space.

We are now at our destination,
In Uranus' new space port
But wait, what's this?
Aliens! Run!

Alastair Campbell (10)
Kenley Primary School

UFO

As the UFO flies through the night
It passes planes while shooting comets out of sight.
It zooms past planets faster than sound
While shooting aliens down to the ground.
He finds his home planet and lands back at home
When he gets there he gets straight on his mobile phone,
To tell his mum the journey's been done.

Thomas Castle (11)
Kenley Primary School

JOURNEY OF THE WHITE HORSES

Wheeling, white waves,
Cave, crashing crests,
Roaring, rock ramming,
Flying fast and floundering fish
Travelling, tossing and teasing
Slinging salt to the shore.

Retreating, reversing, roaring again,
White, whipping, wiping shores clean,
Excitedly exiting, everlasting life
Cleaning, combing crumbs of sand,
Loving, leaping, lapping along lamented locks,
Surveying, salt spraying . . .
    Calm once more.

Madeleine Jones (11)
Kenley Primary School

THE SPIDER

My web is very delicate,
It takes ages to make
So why do people hate it,
It's my home for goodness sake!

My journey round and round it,
Is very tiring,
And when I finally finish,
I stand admiring.

If I could count the webs
That through my life I'd made,
I'd be up to a thousand,
If only I got paid!

Sian Tan (11)
Kenley Primary School

A JOURNEY THROUGH LIFE

If you can stand up for yourself
And never fall down.
If you can bear to hear the truth,
That you have spoken before.
If you can fill the unforgiving second,
With courage and boldness.

If you can wait and not be tired of waiting,
If you are neither friend nor foe,
But keep your distance from whom you may not like,
Then your world will be filled with joy.

Charlotte King (11)
Kenley Primary School

THE KOALA BEAR AND THE MOON

The moon looks down at the smiling koala bear
Who drops her little head to sleep.
She keeps the small figure out of harm,
She keeps her out of reach.
The koala dreams of going to see the moon
She flies through the air the wind whipping through her fur
The stars twinkling as bright as ever,
The koala bear lands in the moon's arms
The moon looks down at the baby koala bear not hearing a peep
Suddenly the moon realises the koala bear is asleep.

Rachael Shanahan (10)
Kenley Primary School

THE SIBERIAN TIGER

The Siberian tiger stalks his prey
An innocent zebra is his victim
He chases it round the jungle clearing
Finally he catches it
He cools off under a tree
With his stomach full.

Gemma Robinson (10)
Kenley Primary School

DINNERS

Monday: cottage pie,
Makes you want to die.

Tuesday: meatballs and spaghetti,
Tastes like confetti.

Wednesday: chicken burger,
Doesn't make you want to go further.

Thursday: roast,
Tastes like rotten toast.

Friday: pizza,
Wait in the playground I'll come and meet ya.

Water's yucky and mucky.

Saturday: yes! KFC,
Makes you want to shout with glee.

Sunday: Oh no, roast,
I feel sick,
Bbbbllllluuuugggghhhh!
Uh oh!

Zoë Kocher (10)
Mytchett Primary School

FUN

'Jump about,
Scream and shout,
All of this is fun.
Laugh and giggle,
Play and tickle,
Everything is fun!'

'What did you say?'
'I said . . .'

'Jump about,
Scream and shout,
All of this is fun.
Laugh and giggle,
Play and tickle,
Everything is fun!'

Lauren Medcalfe (10)
Mytchett Primary School

VOLCANO

The volcano lava is as hot as the sun
It bubbles and plunges to the ground,
Making a thrashing sound,
Like a rhinoceros tumbling down,
And is as delicate as a night gown.

When it explodes it goes eighty feet high,
And when it touches you it makes you die,
It rocks the Earth's core
And people shout with a terrible roar!

And when it's finished it looks like Mars.

Tim Cockrem (11)
Mytchett Primary School

THE MAGIC BOX

I will put in my box . . .
The sparkle of the stars,
The jet black of the night sky,
And the khaki of the grass.

I will put in my box . . .
The sharpness of the shark's tooth,
The glittering gold of the sun,
And the frigid icy frosty ice.

I will put in my box . . .
The blue from the bluest seas,
And the dryness of the desert,
The echo of the mountains.

My box is made of cold fire and hot ice
Mixed to make a good sturdy box.

I will write in my box
All the things I've been dreaming of
And write secrets in the corners,
Then write to the end of my life.

Bradley Pace (10)
Mytchett Primary School

PLAYING

Playing in the garden,
Playing having fun,
Playing with the water hose,
Playing in the sun!

Jumping around in the bedroom,
Jumping on the bed,
Jumping on the pillows,
'Woo hoo!' is what I said!

Jumping up at the table,
Chucking the food on the floor,
I said 'I've had enough thank you,
I don't want any more!'

Lisa Whiting (11)
Mytchett Primary School

THE MAGIC BOX

I will put in the box . . .
The dashing dog dancing all day,
The greedy gorilla grating grains,
The splashing water going down the wishing well.

I will put in my box . . .
The noisy natter of my nan,
The walking snake across the silver sand,
The lion doing the high limbo.

I will put in my box . . .
A gift from a magical hoover,
The big white sparkling teeth of a shark,
The giggle of a snake.

I will put in my box . . .
A whole lump of golden fire,
The powerful toothbrush,
A cat eating rat's cheese.

My box is fashioned by ice hot snow and silver steel,
Moons on the top and stars in the corners,
Its hinges are horseshoes.

I will ride in my box on the second path,
Blow out the candle in my box,
Letting the fire free.

Kerri Simmonds (10)
Mytchett Primary School

THE CRISP GARDEN AND THE COSY HOUSE

The owl hooted suddenly as he saw the glittering snow settling on the
green grass,
The deer looked startled by the frosty plants that had been covered in
snow right under his nose
But inside the house the children sat quietly by the warm fire soaking
in the heat,
While the little mouse sat in his hole feeling the heat from the rusty
brown pipes.

Outside the snowflakes were falling onto the frozen pond
and leafless trees,
The badger scurries away to her cubs nestling in the crumpled leaves,
And the bird is nestling in the roof in the warm feathery nest.

Then all is still, everybody's asleep.

Claire Reah (11)
Mytchett Primary School

WONG, WANG, WING

On my voyage to the
Wong, Wang, Wing
I saw some cows going
Pong, pang, ping.

So I quickly looked back from the
Wong, Wing, Wang
And saw some sheep going
Orangutang!

It couldn't get worse on the
Wing, Wang, Wong
To see my mum wearing
A great big thong!

Austin Surey (10)
Mytchett Primary School

THE MAGIC BOX

I will put in my box . . .
The song of a robin on a winter's eve,
The flip of a fish as it flies for freedom,
A Christmas that never ends.

I will put in my box . . .
A coral from the deepest parts of the Atlantic,
Ice from the top of the top of Mount Everest,
A fire made from snow.

I will put in my box . . .
An immortal soul from the height of all heights,
A star from the farthest of the far reaches of the galaxy,
A second moon and a tenth planet.

I will put in my box . . .
A magpie on the wing,
A snake slithering,
The most chocolatey of chocolate cakes.

My box is fashioned from pure gold,
With magical locks and everlasting walls.

I will fly in my box,
Floating on the up currents of wind and air
I will land at the place where the sea meets the sky.

Christopher McGeehan (9)
Mytchett Primary School

UNICORN

In a faraway place,
Lived a mythical creature,
Its blood was pure,
He was an amazing feature.

Its body was snow-white,
His eyes were perfect blue,
His tail was long and bushy,
Like a squirrel doing Kung Fu.

Its horn is said to be magic,
Although I don't think it's true
It was guarded by gnashing jaws,
It glinted like it was new.

All the people who have tried to find it,
All call it the unseen unicorn
It was too fast for eyes like these,
To see this wonder of Melbourne.

Nicholas Hammond (11)
Mytchett Primary School

THE MAGIC HEART

I will put in my heart . . .
A kiss from my mum and dad,
A smile from a baby,
Laughter from my big sister.

I will put in my heart . . .
The light from the sun,
A crater from the moon,
A twinkle from a star.

I will put in my heart . . .
A pearl from the sea,
A wild wish from a well,
The smell from a rose.

Hayley Evans (10)
Mytchett Primary School

THE MAGIC BOX

I will put in my box . . .
A snake slithering across the silver sand
A horse howling down a hill,
A ship sailing across the seas.

I will put in my box . . .
A lick of a hound,
The wicked laughter of a cruel creature,
A fearful shrieking to the slimy slug.

I will put in my box . . .
A snowman shaking like a jelly,
A devil asking for sweets,
And the sun shining on the sand.

I will put in my box . . .
A wipe of the whistling wand,
A firework fired into the gloomy night,
Papa helping you with your homework.

I shall whiz on my skateboard in the black night.
With the whooshing water too,
With a bat sitting on a broom,
With cursing clouds curled round the broom and I.

Anna Sanders (9)
Mytchett Primary School

THE COBLEWOBLE

The Coblewoble, its eyes like a
Grey murky river, where death
Is edging closer leaping
Out of the water edge.

The deadly whip of a tail
Killing everyone who dares
Try and kill the Coblewoble.

The slimy body covered in vomit
And licking it off for dessert
As a pudding.

The charging through trees,
A herd of elephants charging
For their lives
From the Coblewoble.

His venom sliding outwards
Of the corner of his mouth
He is the king of the beasts.

Its deadly stare is death in an instant
The humans coming to kill.

The jaws and teeth biting,
Chewing, crushing and grinding
Death is upon humans.

Samual Brant (11)
Mytchett Primary School

THE MAGIC BOX

I will put in my box . . .
A dashing dog dancing all night,
A gift from a magical animal,
Some water whooshing going down a well.

I will put in my box . . .
A mischievous monkey making marinades,
A smell from the red roses,
A greedy gorilla grating dry grass.

I will put in my box . . .
A running ravenous river,
A giant tooth from the white shark,
A snake slithering across silver sand.

I will put in my box . . .
A cat eating cat cheese,
The eighth colour of the rainbow,
A silver star in the sun.

My box is fashioned from gold and silver,
With sparkling stars on the lid and secrets in a secret corner
And a little lock with a key.

I shall ski in my box
On the great mountains in Scotland
Then fall to the ground
In the soft white snow.

Victoria Filshie (9)
Mytchett Primary School

DEAD OF AUTUMN

Dead of autumn closing in
Like a sudden sweep of death
Everything still under a steel sky
Falling into deep sleep
But still the squirrels scuttle by
Like the lash of a whip
And the ants marching on their path
Like dots scurrying by with too big loads,
And beetles too, tap, tap, tap,
Like busy workmen laying bricks.

Dead of autumn fastened up
Like a belt round your waist
Still quite warm but nothing moves
'Cept at the dead of night
But still the owl swoops about
Like the faintest whisper on a summer breeze
And the bats are waking in the trees
Like winged mice
And the mice scurry about the house
Like tiny burglars.

Dead of autumn changing round
Like a cold bath
Trees are bare and are offering
No hiding place for creatures
But the last swallows are flying
Like a plane formation
And the woodpeckers are still here
Like a road drill all the day
And the robins hop about
Like a jewel against the snow.

Louise Cooper (10)
Mytchett Primary School

THE DOG

Tail-wagger,
  Walk-tagger,
    Squirrel-chaser,
      Cat-hater,
        Bone-cruncher,
          Meat-muncher,
            Wet-shaker,
              Bone-fetcher,
                Flower-tramper,
                  Mud-stamper,
                    Stick-breaker,
                      Hand-shaker,
                        Wet-licker,
                          Bad-kisser,
                            Cold-nose,
                              Big-toes,
                                Fast-runner,
                              Long-jumper,
                          Mud-flicker,
                        Ball-hitter,
                    Dog-hurtler.

Andrew Warrender (11)
Mytchett Primary School

SWAN

Strong-flapper,
Deep-diver,
Wing-clapper,
Water-skier,
Strong-swimmer.

Ben May (11)
Mytchett Primary School

MY CAT IS A . . .

My cat is a . . .
Fussy-eater,
Night-creeper.

Fur-licker,
Tail-flicker,

Wet-kisser,
Loud-hisser.

Long-sleeper,
Milk-drinker.

Tail-chaser,
Deep scratcher.

Soggy-moggy,
Coat is foggy.

My cat is as fast as a cheetah.

Roxanne Brunswick (10)
Mytchett Primary School

DOG, FROG AND HOG

There once was a dog and a frog and a hog
The frog said 'Come to tea with me and you'll see,
Some scrummy meat and smelly feet.'
So the hog and the dog went to frog's house.
They were trying to keep as quiet as a mouse
Frog's house was in a pond,
Hog wasn't fond of the pond
Dog loved water but dog was shorter than the water
So they couldn't have tea and see the scrummy meat and smelly feet.

Natalie Watkinson (10)
Mytchett Primary School

DON'T

Don't eat fruit on the boot,
Don't put mum in your tum,
Don't be sick on the brick,
And don't be funny with the money,
Don't give a pear to the bear,
And don't chuck a ton at the nun.

Don't let the cat eat the rat,
Don't let the floor touch the door,
Don't tear the beautiful hair,
And don't throw your file in the Nile,
Don't what?
Don't throw your file in the Nile,
Don't what?

Lisa Patterson (10)
Mytchett Primary School

MY POEM

Ting, dong, ting
The clock went ping
And all the people
Went ding, ding, ding
So I went in a boat
Off down the moat
Right past a goat
So I sang
Pling, pong, pang.

David Barlow (9)
Mytchett Primary School

ONOMATOPOEIA VOLCANO

Hot, pot
   Boil, coil,
      Lunge, plunge,
         Rage, wage,
            Leaping, weeping.

Fiery, wiry,
   Brisk, risk,
      Boiling, scalding,
         Flamey, blazey,
            Glowing, lowing,
               Roasting, toasting,
Fast, last,
Extinction!

Catherine Rogers (10)
Mytchett Primary School

DOG

Cold-kisser,
   Called Melissa.
Fast-eater,
   Called Peter.
Nice-taster,
   Quick-sleeper,
Bone-keeper
   Messy-drinker,
Friend-licker,
   Chase their tails
Always pale.

Natalie Logan (11)
Mytchett Primary School

THE TERRIBLE ROCK

There was a young man from China,
Who wasn't a very good climber,
He slipped on a rock and off went his sock,
And that's the man from China.

There was an old man from China,
Who wasn't a very good climber,
He slipped on a rock,
And had a great shock,
And that's the man from China.

There was a middle-aged lady from China,
Who wasn't a very good climber,
She slipped on a rock,
And her clock went tick-tock,
And that's the lady from China.

James Uphill (10)
Mytchett Primary School

MY UNUSUAL DAY

One morning I woke up
I saw my brother wearing a nightie,
My sister was wearing his boxer shorts
They both shouted aaahhh!
My mum woke up soaking wet,
My dad woke up with a jelly on his head,
My grandad woke up halfway down the stairs,
My grandma woke up half bare,
My uncle woke up in the gravel,
My aunty woke up in a frazzle.

Katie Lemon (9)
Mytchett Primary School

SUMMER AND WINTER

Summer and winter are so different.

Summer's colourful,
Beautiful and pretty,
Hot and thrilling,
Juicy fruit is all about,
Nothing else is better than summer.

Winter is dull,
Colours are gone,
Cold and boring,
Shiny leaves fall to the ground,
But then it magically turns to snow!

Stephanie Roberts (10)
Mytchett Primary School

KENNING - DOG

Tail-catcher,
Carpet-scratcher,
Curtain-wrecker,
Big-petter,
Tail-wagger,
Toy-tagger,
Tongue-licker,
Sloppy-kisser,
Scruffy-eater,
Tall-jumper,
Muddy-footer,
Tummy-tickler.

Pennie Glassup (11)
Mytchett Primary School

DON'T

Don't throw a tool at the school,
Don't put Matt near the cat,
Don't let Clive go and dive,
And don't smother Sam in jam!
Don't cover the cap with the map,
And don't give her a worm at the end of term.

Don't put bees near the cheese,
Don't put toffee in the coffee,
Don't put tea in the sea,
And don't throw a spanner at the banner,
Don't throw a spanner at the banner,
Don't what?
Don't throw a spanner at the banner,
Don't what?
Don't throw a spanner at the banner.

Lara Berriman (10)
Mytchett Primary School

THE MAGIC BOX

I will put in my box . . .
A sliding snake on a hot summer's day.

I will put in my box . . .
A champion chess player and a fantasy football player.

I will put in my box . . .
Grumpy gorilla grating grains,
A cat on a mat that is fat,
And blood from a snake.

Joshua Brant (9)
Mytchett Primary School

BEARS AND HARES

Bears and hares don't willingly chase,
No hare or bear has eaten an eclair,
Hares and bears refuse to share,
In fact I think some bears eat hares
Though one day a master bear said to a hare,
'Share your mare'
But this hare said to the bear that he wished not to share his mare.
That night master bear stole the black mare,
And held a gun to the head of that poor creature,
He woke master hare, who at once exclaimed
'Spare the mare! I'll share my mare! I'll share my mare!'
And the bear replied 'Thank you dear hare, for sharing your mare,
I was getting sick of eating pear.'

Suzy Fenge (10)
Mytchett Primary School

HOPE

When I am fifteen years old,
Hope will rise,
For my new pet dog.
The anticipation, the belief, the hope,
For a perfect pet dog.
The desire, the longing is too much to bear,
I must have it now!
My new pet dog
But I must wait,
I must trust my belief,
For my new pet dog.

Alice Surey (10)
Mytchett Primary School

SOUNDS OF FIREWORKS

The rocket sounds like an eagle calling for a mate.
The sparklers sound like an egg in a frying pan.
The Catherine wheel sounds like a hissing snake.
The traffic light releases a red, an amber and a light green.
The other fireworks screech like a car coming to a halt
These magical objects fill the sky with light.

Danny Wheeler (10)
Mytchett Primary School

FRIENDS

Friends are always there,
Friends always care,
Friends always share,
Friends can't bear,
When you're never there.

Corrinne Padwick (9)
Mytchett Primary School

DOLPHIN

Dolphins are an oily, grey and can give a lovely display.

Playing with a small blue ball,
-Gleefully swimming along with a gay smile on his face.

In deep blue fantasy watching this joyful dolphin gliding in a pool.

I'm glad the dolphin is swimming happily.

Nathalie Davy (10)
St Ann's Heath Junior School, Virginia Water

WINTER

W inds blow the leaves off the trees that fall to the ground below,
    making a carpet of red, yellow and brown.
I   ce freezes the plants that have grown,
        the puddles that are in the road,
        ponds in gardens and windows of cars.
N ights get longer the animals sleep in their cosy nests
            waiting for the warmer days of spring.
T   urkey for Christmas, cards to write, presents to wrap
            getting ready for Christmas Day.
E   vergreen trees covered in snow, the land is like a white blanket
            and the children are playing in the snow,
            making a snowman and throwing snowballs
            and having fun in a sledge.
R   ays of sun come from behind the trees, at the break of dawn
            the flowers are shooting
            and the animals are waking,
    I think spring is here!

Katie Neck (9)
St Ann's Heath Junior School, Virginia Water

A HAMSTER

Hamsters store their food in their mouths.
Hamsters twitch their whiskers.
Hamsters sit in your hand.
Hamsters run around in their wheel.
Hamsters have a nap in the day.
Hamsters are cute and cuddly.
Hamsters have different colour patches.
Hamsters curl up tight in a ball.

Lara Day (10)
St Ann's Heath Junior School, Virginia Water

MARK THE SHARK

There was a shark
Called Mark,
He lived in an ark,
In the dark.

His teeth
Were sharp,
He liked eating beef.

In May
He sleeps all day
In June he says
What a wonderful lay.

Nicola Bean (8)
St Ann's Heath Junior School, Virginia Water

MY BROTHER

My horrid brother
He always goes and hugs Mother
If I have beaten him again
On another computer game.
Some people think he's cute
But I think he's a right brute
He always gets attention
And when I get tense
I fine him fifty pence
Of course he says no
And tells me to go
And get a life!

Anna Morrison (10)
St Ann's Heath Junior School, Virginia Water

ALIENS

Aliens are here
The rest are very near,
No one knows what they look like
One could be on a bike
The army are ready
They hold their guns very steady
The aliens approach
The leader looks like a cockroach
A big war starts
And people start throwing darts.
The aliens have their laser guns
One starts eating buns
Suddenly it ends
People have to build dens
The aliens say goodbye
Goodbye friends.

Jake McGuire (10)
St Ann's Heath Junior School, Virginia Water

TOUCH

Touch - what can you feel?

The tall prickly spines of a hedgehog,
The silky fur of a black and white cat,
The velvet soft petals of a pink pansy.

The cool cotton pillow on a warm summer's night,
The smooth skin of a baby's face,
The warmth of a hug at the end of the day.

Isobel McNeill (8)
St Ann's Heath Junior School, Virginia Water

HAVE YOU HEARD ABOUT MY TEACHER?

Have you heard about my teacher?
She is really one loud screecher
Though she is very kind
But she does know how to blow our minds
She gives hard and easy work to do in fifteen mins
And when we're doing RE she's always talking us into being sins
Now we're onto Saxon towns
And she's saying they're all around
I just don't know why she's so weird
Then she's telling us a story but only once we're cleared
I know this might sound weird but
That's my teacher.

Harriet McGuire (9)
St Ann's Heath Junior School, Virginia Water

MY CAT

In the evening
My cat comes upstairs
She hops on my bed
If she sees my feet
She'll dart and pounce
Until she's satisfied
That she's caught her prey
She stretches out along my legs
And rests her head on my stomach
Until I get squashed
And shoo her away.

Jack Foster (9)
St Ann's Heath Junior School, Virginia Water

STORM

A storm is loud,
A storm has rain,
I think the world has gone insane.

The lightning strikes,
And flashes with power,
The rain is now more than a shower.

The wind is strong,
The wind is bold,
It blows down people that are old.
It blows down fences,
It blows down trees,
It rocks the boats upon the seas.

I hate storms,
I want them to go,
I would rather have
Some
Thick, white, snow.

Harry Matthews (9)
St Ann's Heath Junior School, Virginia Water

SPRING

Spring is here, how can we tell
Because the leaves begin to uncurl,
Little shoots from deep beneath the ground
Poke out their heads towards the light,
From their long winter sleep little creatures awake
Lots of newborn animals are to be seen,
Fluffy clouds, brighter skies, longer days getting warmer
All of these say that spring is on its way.

Antony Capes (9)
St Ann's Heath Junior School, Virginia Water

SNOW

Winter is cold,
Winter is blowy,
Winter is chilly,
But most of all it's snowy.

Snowflakes fall on the top of my nose,
Hats, gloves and scarves are the perfect clothes.

Kids in the park have a snowball fight,
The snow on the mountain tops are a beautiful sight.

It's lovely and warm inside by the fire,
But outside where the snow is, is the place to admire.

Whatever the weather, wherever you go,
In the wintertime there is always snow.

Gemma Moore (10)
St Ann's Heath Junior School, Virginia Water

SEASONS OF THE YEAR

Spring is when new animals are born,
Did you know some like to eat corn?

Summer is when the sun shines bright,
Just like a little candlelight.

Autumn is when the leaves are flying,
And because of that the birds are sighing.

Winter is when the snowflakes are falling,
And when the insects are not crawling.

Fiona Everington (8)
St Ann's Heath Junior School, Virginia Water

NATURE

Nature is good,
Insects have food,
Worms and snails,
And other males.

Lots of insects you can pick,
Lots of them you can flick,
Butterflies can fly,
But they don't really spy.

Insects see things,
But they don't tread on pins,
There are big long trees,
And lots of small leaves.

Petra Aryiku (10)
St Ann's Heath Junior School, Virginia Water

MY SECRET GARDEN

Roses, tulips, daffodils everywhere,
A carved swing swaying in the breeze.
A bridge wrapped in ivy,
And all kinds of birds singing in the trees.
I look out of my garden,
Over the old stone wall.
I see the distant playground, where children shout and climb,
I hear the noisy cars go past.
In my garden there is no noise,
Only the sound of the fountains and the crystal stream go by.
The gentle whisper of the breeze and the singing of the birds,
As they flap their wings and fly.

Helen Moggridge (10)
St Ann's Heath Junior School, Virginia Water

WINTER

W hite snow covers the land,
I t's like the icy North Pole,
N oisy children playing in the snow,
T eeth chattering as the snowfalls,
E ven though it's freezing cold rabbits come out to play,
R unning children in the snow wish it's the same all year round.

Michelle Green (11)
St Ann's Heath Junior School, Virginia Water

THE UNKNOWN CREATURE

The unknown creature stalks about in the night
With all his strength and might.
When anyone comes near his grave, he says,
'I'm the unknown, I'm dead'
He lives in a cave under a grave
So don't go near the grave or we won't see you again.

Amelia Clarke (9)
St Ann's Heath Junior School, Virginia Water

DOLPHINS

I love dolphins, they swim like me
I wish I had a pet dolphin called Lee.
Lee, like all dolphins is very clever
We will be friends forever and ever.

Katie Morris (8)
St Ann's Heath Junior School, Virginia Water

MOVIES

Scary movies,
Funny movies,
Weird movies,
Baby movies and
Nice movies.
They are really all the same
I like funny movies the best.

Scary moves,
Funny movies,
Weird movies,
Baby movies and
Nice movies.
None of them scares me
Except if there's a mummy.

Melanie Wright (9)
St Ann's Heath Junior School, Virginia Water

CONCENTRATION CAMP

'Women to the right,
Men to the left.'
The newly captured prisoners joined the lines of death.
'Twins wanted over here!'
The twins walked over shaking with fear.
They joined the queue to be experimented on.
Captured till the war was won.
They never saw each other again
The prisoned Jewish women and men.

Laura Tayler (11)
St Ann's Heath Junior School, Virginia Water

READY FOR SCHOOL

When I wake up in the morning
And I try to get dressed
All I can hear is yawning
I want to lay down and rest
I have my breakfast
Clean my teeth and do my hair
Hurry up or you'll never get there.
I get into the car
And in no time at all
I didn't go far
And now I'm at school.
The day has just begun
English, science, maths and sums.

Cara Vaisey (10)
St Ann's Heath Junior School, Virginia Water

COLOURS

Black is found in the darkest cave,
Blue is found on the wettest wave,
Red is found in the sunset sky,
Green is found on the trees so high,
Pink is found on the cleanest pig,
Brown is found on a log or a twig,
All of these colours are in our sight,
From grey to yellow all so bright,
Maybe some day we will make some more,
Because they're the most beautiful things I ever saw.

Sophie Clarke (11)
St Ann's Heath Junior School, Virginia Water

MY MONKEY COLLECTION

I have apes
Of all shapes,
A hairy gorilla,
Who is quite a thriller.
A lady gibbon,
Covered in ribbons.

I've an orang-utan
Who hangs.
Furry chimpanzees
With bony knees,
And a baby baboon
Who sings squeaky tunes.
And during the night
We all snuggle up tight!

Helen Jenkins (8)
St Ann's Heath Junior School, Virginia Water

CHRISTMAS TIME

Christmas, Christmas, Christmas,
Christmas is almost here.
Christmas, Christmas, Christmas,
Dads are drinking beer.
Christmas, Christmas, Christmas,
Presents are under the tree.
Christmas, Christmas, Christmas,
Christmas has come for me.

Jennifer Davy (8)
St Ann's Heath Junior School, Virginia Water

THE SEASONS

S pring is the first season,
E ach little flower will grow,
A baby bird in a nesting box
S ummer is here now I know
O h I hope it doesn't rain this year,
N ice holidays by the sea,
S un and sand to play in.

A n ice cream just for me!
R eal fun collecting conkers
E very other day.

D id you find a winner?
I' ll give you a match I say!
F ind that autumn is now gone,
F un playing in the snow,
E veryone knows winter has come
R udolph and Santa will come and go!
E vening draws on, on New Year's Eve,
N obody can wait,
T omorrow it will be a new year.

Jennifer Shelley (8)
St Ann's Heath Junior School, Virginia Water

WINTER

W hite snow as far as you can see,
I cicles melting in the tree.
N uts are ready to be cooked,
T o see the footprints if you look!
E veryone is playing in the snow
R ipe fruits have to go.

Laura Dossett (9)
St Ann's Heath Junior School, Virginia Water

SCIENCE LIFE

Science, science, lots of fun
You get to experiment on lots of dung.
Test tubes, droppers, stirrers and bangs,
All add up to the science lab.

Making potions, bubble, bubble,
Lots of colours, purple, purple
What do we know?
What do we need?
Got to get the fungi seed,
What about the fungi feed?

Rebecca Bean (10)
St Ann's Heath Junior School, Virginia Water

BEST FRIENDS

A best friend is kind to you
They cheer you up when you're feeling blue.

They meet you at school, do games and play
They keep you happy - any day.

Danielle, Max - any name,
Skipping, running - any game.

Ugly, pretty, dumb or clever
A boy, a girl - a best friend forever!

Emma Laing (9)
St Ann's Heath Junior School, Virginia Water

OLD ROBIN REDBREAST

The robin doesn't come in summer,
He only comes in winter and spring.
The children like to race outside,
To clearly hear him sing!

Here we go again talking,
About old Robin Redbreast.
His tummy's brightly coloured,
It's better than the rest!

The only bird that can sing so nice,
Is the wonderful Robin Redbreast.
His tune is like an angel's song,
It's better than the rest!

Joy Hunt (8)
St Ann's Heath Junior School, Virginia Water

WAITING

Waiting, waiting, waiting
For snow and ice to appear.
Waiting, waiting, waiting,
As winter disappears.

Waiting, waiting, waiting,
Waiting for time to come.
Waiting, waiting, waiting
For the summer sun.

Daniel Norris (8)
St Ann's Heath Junior School, Virginia Water

TOUCH

Touch!
What can you feel?

The feel of a chick,
The feel of a stick,
The touch of a tick,
The feel of a flick.

Touch!
What can you feel?

The feel of a blistering snake,
The touch of a flake,
The feel of a cake,
The touch of a steak.

Jonathan Miller (8)
St Ann's Heath Junior School, Virginia Water

THE DOLPHIN

Dolphin, dolphin over the sea
What can you see?
Can you see a bumblebee
Or are you having a cup of tea?
I can see a flea
And it looks like it's having a cup of tea
Or is it a bee?
I can't quite see
But maybe you can see
Just maybe.

Rebecca Kelly (8)
St Ann's Heath Junior School, Virginia Water

THE OCEAN

The ocean is big, the ocean is small, however did God make us all.
He made us big, He made us small, however we are good or bad,
God loves us all.
He made animals big, He made animals small, however animals are
God loves them all.
He made a giraffe big, He made a giraffe small, however giraffes are
God loves them all.
He made an elephant big, He made an elephant small, however
elephants are
God loves them all.
He made a zebra big, He made a zebra small, however zebras are
God loves them all.
He made us big, He made us small, however we look
God loves us all.

Charlotte MacKenzie (7)
St Ann's Heath Junior School, Virginia Water

OLIVER

Oliver is a dog
Who is very cute.
He cuddles me
When I am alone
I love my Oliver
Because he loves me
When I come to give him a treat
He always says woof, woof
He is always fun to play with
Because I love him.

Hayley Hedges (7)
St Ann's Heath Junior School, Virginia Water

A RESTLESS DREAMER

Pow, crash, boom!
A big black baboon
Sailed past my window . . .
On a journey to the moon.

'Would you like some cheese?'
'Meow, yes please!'
My cat likes milk . . .
And honey from the bees.

Closer comes the badger,
You almost think he's had-ya
For his tea . . .
You wouldn't want that, would-ya?

Abigail Houghton (11)
St Ann's Heath Junior School, Virginia Water

WILD RABBIT

Wild rabbit hopping free
Under bushes through the tree
Nearly there, here at last
Home in my burrow eating fast.

Now it's time for me to go to bed
I lay down my sleepy head
Now I'm dreaming of a vegetable patch
Carrots, cabbages, what a lovely batch.

Lucy Morris (8)
St Ann's Heath Junior School, Virginia Water

LONELY HEARTS

Fun-loving troll, dirty and smelly
With damp, slimy skin and big hairy belly,
Nice muddy fingers and grubby, wet toes,
Hot, steamy breath and rings through each nose.

With stains on his shirt and holes in his socks,
Teeth that need cleaning and knots in his locks,
Tears in his trousers and scuffs on his shoes,
He's waiting to meet someone lovely like you.

He likes dirty ditches and hiding in holes,
Is certain to win when he fights other trolls,
Is very attentive, will woo you with roses,
After he's used them to pick both his noses.

He lives on his own, in a dark stinking pit,
Oozing with slime and covered in spit,
Now feeling lonely, he hopes there's a chance
He can meet someone similar for fun and romance.

Levi Draper-Smith (10)
St Ann's Heath Junior School, Virginia Water

WINTER HAS ARRIVED

W inter has arrived
I   t's cold, wet and windy
N othing seems to grow
T he nights are longer and darker
E very leaf falls off the trees
R ain never seems to go.

Jack Milnes (8)
St Ann's Heath Junior School, Virginia Water

MY TEACHER

My teacher is cool,
We can't call her a fool.
Marking all our work,
Never going berserk.

My teacher is never late for school,
Doesn't like any pupil to drool
But could you imagine if
My teacher was late for school.

We'd have an awful day,
We couldn't work or play
This is what would happen if she was late for school,
And my teacher wouldn't be so cool!

Laura Stephens (11)
St Ann's Heath Junior School, Virginia Water

SCHOOL

I wish I didn't have to go to school,
Then I could go shopping in the mall.
I'd play on my computer every day and night,
Watching my sims fight, fight, fight.
I think I would get board of that,
So I would play with the cat.
If I didn't have to go to school,
My vocabulary would definitely fall.

Tiffany Ellson (10)
St Ann's Heath Junior School, Virginia Water

MY DOG

My dog is very nice if you stroke him twice.
He will bark if you take him to the park.
If you give him a squeaky toy he will be a good boy.
If you give him food
He won't be in a bad mood.
If he wants to play
He will play in every way.

Bethany Holmes (8)
St Ann's Heath Junior School, Virginia Water

A SNAIL

A snail always likes the ground,
A snail slithers all around.
They leave behind them a silvery trail
A slime which comes from their tail.
I like snails on a leaf
But when they get caught I feel such grief.

Hannah Maunder (7)
St Ann's Heath Junior School, Virginia Water

TRAFFIC

T raffic is a hateful thing
R oads are filled with cars
A t 6am the rush hour begins
F umes belching out their chemical harm
F antastically we all take part
I n polluting the air we breathe
C ome on now, let's think again of the world we'd like to see.

Dominic Shine (8)
St Ann's Heath Junior School, Virginia Water

PLAYING IN THE GARDEN

Pretty flowers,
Lots of colours,
Orange, yellow, pink and purple.
Never hurt them as you hurtle
Past them on your bike.
Swing up high,
To the sky,
Come down low
Don't be slow,
For there's lots of games to play
In our garden.

Abigail Gaskin (7)
St Ann's Heath Junior School, Virginia Water

CATS

Siamese cats,
Manx cats,
Black cats,
White cats,
Pink fluffy, friendly cats,
Fat cats,
Slim cats,
Spotted cats,
Striped cats,
Grey, ugly, nasty cats.

Emma Graham (9)
St Ann's Heath Junior School, Virginia Water

116

FEEL THE FLOW!

I start as a trickle,
Moving slow,
As I grow bigger
Watch me go,
Swiftly meandering
Through the cold,
I'm getting wider,
Big and bold.
In my path
A tree's root lay,
I bubble over them
Throughout the day,
I see the public,
Stop and stare,
I don't mind as long
As they take care.
I pass marshy areas,
And lots of paths,
All the birds hear me,
Tinkle and laugh,
I take care of the wildlife
And save them from thirst,
I don't reach the sea,
But I do expand
From a little river
To form a lake!
So now when you pollute,
You know I'm for your sake.

Marie Elsdon (10)
St Ann's Heath Junior School, Virginia Water

CHRISTMAS POEM

A is for angel, shining in the sky,
B is for berries, all bright red, that just lie,
C is for candles, flickering to make light,
D is for dinner, at night,
E is for epiphany, for when wise men came,
F is for fire, all bright red flame,
G is for goose, white like snow,
H is for holly, its leaves all aglow,
I is for ice, hanging off trees,
J is for Jesus, who taught us to say please,
K is for kiss, under the mistletoe,
L is for lamb, so sweet and slow,
M is for mistletoe, hanging up nicely,
N is for nativity, about Jesus precisely,
O is for ornaments, nicely laid on the shelf,
P is for presents, on the floor for myself,
Q is for quiver, when you've opened a present,
R is for Rudolph, happy and pleasant,
S is for snow, all squidgy and white,
T is for tinsel, on the Christmas tree bright,
U is for unwrapped, Christmas paper,
V is for very tired, after Christmas later,
W is for wrappings, all over the floor,
X is for Xmas, waiting to come through the door,
Y is for Yule log, after everyone's fed,
Z is for tired children off to bed!
    Zzzzz.

Natasha Day (8)
St Ann's Heath Junior School, Virginia Water

THE SCARY DRAGON

Dragons are fierce fighters
Dangerous glaring eyes
He is an armoured roarer
Ears like mountains
Feet like houses
His breath is as hot as a bonfire
His claws dig into the ground
He sounds like an earthquake
His teeth are like knives
To tear into his enemies.

Harriet Plummer (8)
St Catherine's Primary School, Bletchingley

DRAGONS

Dragons, dragons hunting day and night.
Their eyes are X-rays hunting you down.

Beware, beware dragons are there!
They're round every corner and everywhere!

Beware, beware dragons *are there!*

Rebecca Simpson (8)
St Catherine's Primary School, Bletchingley

THE SHY SPIDER

In my cupboard up high
Lives a spider very shy
He eats all the food
When he's in a grumpy mood.

Charlotte McGinn (9)
St Catherine's Primary School, Bletchingley

DRAGON

Dangerous killers, eaters,
Killing devil, gigantic, furious, horn-tailed, fire-breathing
      bone crunchers,
Teeth gnashers, petrifying roarers,
Fearless lizards, dagger-like claws, blood eyes.
Snotty snorter, grumpy stomper, munching flesh-eaters,
Stress flyers, bright, angry, terrifying, fierce
Scaly treasure protector, living in a rocky mountain.

Rainer Smith (8)
St Catherine's Primary School, Bletchingley

THE GODZILER

In my cupboard there lay a spider
A scary, hairy spider
It likes biting people to make them squeal
And never cares how they feel
He runs around and laughs for ever
And he thinks he's very clever.

Gwendolyn Smith (8)
St Catherine's Primary School, Bletchingley

DRAGON

D   agger-like claws with silver paws
R   ed bloodshot eyes, snorting smoke
A   n angry face is a big disgrace
G   leaming fire from his mouth
O   range body from the sun
N   obody will go near him.

Rebecca Silk (8)
St Catherine's Primary School, Bletchingley

DRAGONS

D ragons are the most dangerous creatures,
R oaring and flapping its big windy wings
A ngry fire bubbles in its belly so large and hot
G orgeous scales shimmer in the light
O riental monster stomping day and night
N auseating lizard causing such a fright!

Chloe Phipps (8)
St Catherine's Primary School, Bletchingley

DRAGON

D angerous fire-breathing lizard,
R oaring, gigantic creature,
A ngry meat-eater,
G rumpy stomper,
O ne X-ray eye, red spot glaring,
N ine sharp teeth, crunching and biting.

Emily Field (9)
St Catherine's Primary School, Bletchingley

A SPIDER IN THE CUPBOARD

In my cupboard way up high,
Lives a spider very shy,
He eats the food,
But never cares,
He's very mean and never shares,
He says it's never fair it's always cold,
And in three years time he'll be very old.

Emma Booth (8)
St Catherine's Primary School, Bletchingley

DRAGON

D eadly roarer crawling through the forest
R ooting trees while creeping roughly
A mber eyes staring at everyone
G igantic fire-breather breathing on his prey
O dour breath flowing from his humungous mouth
N aked fire blazing from a distance.

Sarah Sheen (8)
St Catherine's Primary School, Bletchingley

DRAGON

D ragons are the most fiercest fiends,
R oaring and flapping their great big wings.
A rrowing about their great big eyes looking at things,
   Count to three and then they're gone - history.
G orgeous iridescent scales,
O n their huge armoured bodies,
N o one ever sees them.

Kitty Kinder (9)
St Catherine's Primary School, Bletchingley

DRAGON

D eep in the forest lives a bloodshot bone-crusher,
R oars like a deadly treasure protector,
A ngry, with dagger-like claws.
G hostly roar the evil things has,
O bviously fire-breathing, gnasher thing,
N ewt-eating, fire-breathing, bone-crusher thing.

Charlotte Harris (8)
St Catherine's Primary School, Bletchingley

THE BIG LOTTERY WIN

There was once man, who was so poor,
His house didn't even have a door.
He gathered up all his money,
And got a lottery ticket from his old friend, Sonny.
He hoped he would win,
Before he put it in the bin.
Today was his lucky day
But he didn't want to say
Because his friends would want some cash
And he would have to quickly dash.
He wanted to spend his winnings,
So he started from the beginnings.
He made up his mind on a mansion in France,
Where he would sing and dance.
There he lived some happy days
And the bills were easy to pay.

Katie Slater & Dorothy Yau (11)
St Elpheges RC Junior School, Wallington

I HAVE A DALMATIAN

I have a Dalmatian that has lots of spots,
I have a Dalmatian that can draw lots of dots.
I have a Dalmatian that plays all day,
I have a Dalmatian that's good and gay.
I have a Dalmatian that goes out at night,
I have a Dalmatian that shines in the light.
When I go out my Dalmatian will follow behind,
But I don't care and I don't mind.

Vanessa Richter (7)
St Elpheges RC Junior School, Wallington

EASTER

Isn't Easter so yummy
With all the chocolate eggs and bunnies?
This is when chicks hatch,
Batch by batch by batch.
If at Easter it was sunny,
I think all the bees would make some honey.
But don't forget the true Easter,
Or you might just hear about it from your teacher.

Karrie Colfer (10)
St Elpheges RC Junior School, Wallington

WINTER

Lake, glistening, while the moonlight shines down on it . . .
Snow, gleaming, making the world look whiter than unicorns . . .
Moon, making sure everything is gleaming white by nightfall . . .

Winter!

What would we do without the glistening, gleaming, white world . . .?

Alexander Slater (10)
St Elpheges RC Junior School, Wallington

UNTITLED

In the garden, underneath the tree,
That's where Hitler sleeps like a bee,
All the children smile with glee,
In the garden, underneath the tree!

Nichola Louis (10)
St Elpheges RC Junior School, Wallington

THE TEST

Revision for tests are really annoying,
Revision for tests are really destroying.
It destroys your time,
Playing time, and sleeping time.

If we all go to our classes,
We'll all get very good passes.
But the studying at home,
Means we've got to be alone,
Which is not what I like.

I wish we didn't have to do tests,
Because they really are pests.
But having a test is for your own good,
It will better your prospects
And so it should.

Melissa Strachan (11)
St Elpheges RC Junior School, Wallington

FRIENDS

Friends, friends
Happy friends
Fat friends
Skinny friends
And tall friends
They are all kind
And helpful to us
Even when we make a fuss
They are always looking after us
When we fall over and hurt our knees
They never come and tease
But always try to please

Maeve Hickey (8)
St Elpheges RC Junior School, Wallington

THE MAGIC WOOD

You must not go to the woods at night
Because there is no light.
Do not moan
You're not alone.

I met a man
His hair like a fan.
His clothes were sewn
He looked as old as ancient Rome
But he was not alone.

In the trees and behind the bush
Were little eyes, gone in a whoosh!
I hear the wolves howl
But there's a monster on the prowl.

Just then I think I see
Lurking behind a tree
Eyes of green
Breath of steam
I run!

You must not go to the woods at night
Because there is no light.
Do not moan
You're not alone.

Liam Brooks (9)
St Elpheges RC Junior School, Wallington

GREEDY DOG

This dog will eat anything!
Apple core and bacon fat,
Milk you poured out for the cat.
He likes the string that ties the roast
And relishes hot buttered toast.
Hide your chocolate! He's a thief!
He'll even eat your handkerchief.
And if you don't like sudden shocks,
Carefully conceal your socks.
Leave some soup without a lid,
You'll wish you never did.
When you think he must be full,
You find him gobbling bits of wool,
Orange peel or paper bags,
Dusters and old cleaning rags.

This dog will eat anything,
Except for mushrooms and cucumbers!

Virginie Kukanathan (8)
St Elpheges RC Junior School, Wallington

OUR PETS

O   ur pets aren't all the same;
U   gly, pretty, wild and tame.
R   abbits, fish, dogs and cats,

P   hillip even has two bats!
E   lephants are far too big,
T   o run and chase and to play tig.
S   haring love with our pets . . . is *best*

Lindsey Bayley (10)
St Joseph's Catholic Primary School, Redhill

WOOD GNOME

Behind a bush what do I see?
A wood gnome looking at me.
A long beard, a cheeky grin,
Wood gnome who looks so very thin.
Won't you be my friend and let me see what you do therein?
Around him wildlife, forest and ponds,
All so pretty with magical sound.
He looks after birds' nests for birds around
And knows all their sounds.
Up goes the wood gnome lift, high in the trees
And looks at the busy wasps and bees.
He only picks rare flowers for medicine.
Within he really has a busy life
With little time to rest a while.
So goodbye my friend, for now
I'll visit again for a gnome know-how.

Gabriella Clarke (8)
St Joseph's Catholic Primary School, Redhill

IN HONOUR OF POETS

I tip my hat to A A Milne,
Spike Milligan too,
'Cause they can write a poem,
Which is more than I can do.

I think and think for hours,
But nothing seems quite right.
I sit at my desk and stare at the page,
All day long and into the night

And when I think I've hit it,
The words don't look like they should.
It seems almost impossible,
To write something any good!

So I tip my hat to A A Milne,
Spike Milligan too,
'Cause they can write a poem,
Which is more than I can do.

Sylvia Rose Bishop (10)
St Joseph's Catholic Primary School, Redhill

SLOW BUT SURE

Slowly as the tortoise runs,
Elegantly as the ants crawl,
Slow but sure,
There is something changing,
But what, it's a mystery,
To me.

Majestically as the plane flies,
Rapidly as the fire strengthens,
The more I investigate the wider my knowledge,
Still I do not know.

In the library day and night,
Though now, I'm top in English,
And I've learnt my *ABC's*
I look up to the stars and think and think and think,
What is it?

Florence Wallace (10)
St Joseph's Catholic Primary School, Redhill

WRITER'S BLOCK

I think I've caught
Writer's block off my friend
My head's turned into a cube,
I haven't got a single idea
And my writing hand won't move.

My ideas have stowed away
On the latest ship,
For my unwanted thoughts,
It is definitely
Writer's block that I've caught.

Hang on! Wait a tick!
I've just realised,
I'm actually writing a poem!
I think the strange shape of my head
Is slowly, but surely going.

So I've been cured
Of that horrible virus.
(The virus called writer's block)
Oh no! I've run out of ideas again,
I'm afraid I'll have to stop.

Jennifer Spragg (10)
St Joseph's Catholic Primary School, Redhill

CINQUAIN

Listen
With the wind's tones
On a shiny evening
Do you notice the flowers move
And sway?

Harriet Taylor (10)
St Joseph's Catholic Primary School, Redhill

THERE'S DOGS HERE TO BE SEEN

There's dogs here to be seen
There's dogs here to be seen
You hear these noises when
There's dogs here to be seen
You hear . . .
    Woof!
      Woof!
        Swish
          Swish
            Whimper
              Whimper

They ask you to play
Or have a walk
But all you say is . . .
    'Stop it please!'
      'We have no time.'
      'Not now.'

Joanna Sadler (8)
St Joseph's Catholic Primary School, Redhill

IN THE FOG

In the fog
I grumble
and rumble
inside,
I tumble over
and then I mumble,
when is the fog going
to go?

Louise Cook (7)
St Joseph's Catholic Primary School, Redhill

DAFFODILS

Daffodils trumpeting silently,
Swaying in the breeze.
Bright as the sunshine,
Sparkling with dew,
Dainty like a ballerina,
Beckoning in the spring.
They're always there on St David's Day,
Gallantly standing there against the rain,
Dancing
    Trumpeting
      Swaying
        Bright
          Sparkling
        Dainty
      Beckoning
    Gallant.

Elizabeth A R Flynn (9)
St Joseph's Catholic Primary School, Redhill

THE NEW CAT

Stretched out on the couch so small,
Playing with her tiny ball.
She doesn't like the swimming pool!
She has a habit,
Of chasing rabbit.
When it's night,
She wraps up tight.
Dead rats on the floor,
Blood and bone by the door.

Stephanie Barnes (10)
St Joseph's Catholic Primary School, Redhill

I WENT ON A JOURNEY

I went on a journey, a journey to space,
The moon was so bright that it lit up my face,
I looked down to the Earth below and said, 'My goodness,
It looks so small, it is smaller than space.'
I went back down in my rocket from space and forgot all about space.

But the very next day I went on a journey, a journey to space,
I saw six aliens who were dancing in space,
They jumped in my rocket where I was thinking about Mars,
We zoomed on to Mars where they gave me Mars bars,
When they weren't looking I jumped in my rocket
And zoomed through the stars,
When I landed I opened the bars
And had a surprise as they were made of stars.

Lily Lovegrove-Saville (7)
St Joseph's Catholic Primary School, Redhill

ALL ABOUT HENRY VIII

Henry VIII was very fat,
He still managed to fit a hat.
Henry married six wives
But hardly any of them survived.
He loved to eat,
Especially meat!
He killed a lot,
The weather was usually hot.
Henry ruined loads of churches,
He had loads of purses.
So now you know about Henry VIII,
So don't go and put on weight!

Joe Stephen Filgate (10)
St Joseph's Catholic Primary School, Redhill

FOUR SEASONS

Summer's here, off we go
On our holiday to Spain.
Looking forward to the beach,
Hope to see my friends again.

Here comes autumn twirling in,
Leaves at your feet.
Red, brown, yellow and orange,
What a pretty sight to see.

Next comes winter, wrap up warm,
Christmas nearly here.
Sparkling angels top the Christmas tree,
Decorations everywhere.

Here comes spring,
Bleating lambs,
Chirping birds,
Blossom on the branches.

But most of all let's celebrate
Jesus rose again.

Nicole Tootill (10)
St Joseph's Catholic Primary School, Redhill

LIVING THINGS

Bump, stomp, bump, stomp
An elephant
Grump, clump, grump, clump
A rhino
Gossip, pollution, gossip, pollution
A human.

Aimee Castles-Greene (10)
St Joseph's Catholic Primary School, Redhill

PIGS!

Pigs are cute
Pigs are clever
They like their food
And they like the weather

They rush to their troughs
When they smell food
They push to the front
And are ever so rude!

They have great big snouts
And curly pink tails
They like bathing in mud
And camping in Wales.

Georgina Bryne-Eccles (8)
St Joseph's Catholic Primary School, Redhill

PIANO LESSONS

I love to sit down and play
It makes my bad thoughts go away
I play the piano today
The people don't go away

I play a lot of tunes
I started to learn in June
I can read the music notes
And my family give me their votes
They all tell me I'm quite good
It's because I practice like I should!

Phillip Taylor (8)
St Joseph's Catholic Primary School, Redhill

JOURNEYS

Journeys, journeys left and right.
Which one shall I take tonight?

Over the hills and far away.
Will it be an adventurous day?

Over the lands,
And across the sands.

Bobbing on the seas,
Blown by the breeze.

Through the clouds in the sky,
Along with the birds I can fly.

Swinging through the jungle up in the trees,
Or down below creeping on my knees.

Watching the stars from a desert tent.
Camels sleep with their knees bent.

Hippopotamus splashing about.
Crocodiles snapping. *Watch out!*

Butterflies fluttering in the air.
Bumblebees buzzing everywhere.

Polar bears travelling in the snow.
Where are they going? I don't know.

Journeys when I'm asleep and when I'm awake.
I wonder what journeys today I will make?

Georgina Stone (8)
St Joseph's Catholic Primary School, Redhill

SEA

Through the night it creeps
As a cat
Ready to pounce
On this and that

Scared, it creeps back
Then on again
So unsure
It doesn't know what to do

It gulps
It swallows tiny grains of sand
Rising and sinking
Onward it goes with its journey

Jessica Price (9)
St Joseph's Catholic Primary School, Redhill

THE SEASONS

Summer is light
Summer is bright

Autumn is damp
So turn on your lamp

Winter is cold
It makes you feel old

Spring is bright
So you won't get a fright

Sarah Finlayson (10)
St Joseph's Catholic Primary School, Redhill

THE DRAGON THAT WAS NEITHER FRIEND NOR FOE

In the Chines caves,
Where no one dared to go,
There lived a fierce, fire-breathing dragon,
He was neither friend nor foe.

One day a Chinese warrior,
Was sent away to go,
To kill the fierce, fire-breathing dragon,
That was neither friend nor foe.

When the brave Chinese warrior,
Got to where he was meant to go,
He found the fire-breathing dragon,
And the dragon said, 'Hello!'

The warrior fled from the cave,
Shouting, 'Help me - oh no!'
He had left the fire-breathing dragon,
That was a friend not a foe.

Alexander James Gant (10)
St Joseph's Catholic Primary School, Redhill

I'M SORRY

I'm sorry that I hurt you,
Up the stairs I go,
I cry, cry, cry,
Down the stairs I go,
Mum and God I'm sorry,
I love you lots and lots,
Thank you for forgiving me,
I'll be the best I can.

Mhairi Kirkaldy (9)
St Joseph's Catholic Primary School, Redhill

THE ANGEL'S CRY FOR FREEDOM

Her eyes glitter with piercing colours through the moonlight beam,
As she weeps a cry for freedom.
Only silver silence can be heard,
The winter's evening breeze flutters past her cheeks
As silent tears slide down her tender face.
She smiles blissfully to the skylit planet of the elegant moon beyond,
For there she stands patiently upon the calmed lake
Forever . . . waiting . . . waiting and waiting
Until we meet again.

Alexandra Knowles (9)
St Joseph's Catholic Primary School, Redhill

APPLE

Red, like a fire burning in the grate,
Sparkling with colours of joy,
Red, like a lion's roar,
Its colour sitting and waiting for danger to pass by,
Shining like the glittering earth.

Its core is like a spiky cactus, full of mystery and moist,
Cracking with joy,
Juicy and slimy, full of use,
Quivering with haste,
Full of happy faces,

Full of mysterious treasures,
Undressed, waiting for another life.

Lilli McGeehan (9)
St Paul's RC Primary School, Thames Ditton

POEM ABC

A is for apple
B is for baseball
C is for cat
D is for diamond
E is for eye
F is for fungus
G is for giraffe
H is for hair
I is for Irish wolfhound
J is for Jackstone
K is for keeper
L is for life
M is for miles
N is for nothing
O is for outboard
P is for pencil
Q is for queen
R is for rod
S is for safe
T is for table tennis
U is for upright
V is for video
W is for walk
X is for xylophone
Y is for Yorkshire pudding
Z is for zoo.

Hannah Sullivan (10)
St Paul's RC Primary School, Thames Ditton

SMELLS

Bread just cooked in the oven,
As for biscuits, I just love them,
The sea is going in and out,
Petrol from the cars about,
Ice cream from the corner shop,
New wood that has just been chopped,
Chocolate is a really nice dream,
A cake with lovely double cream,
Hot dogs roasting on the spot,
Apple pie nice and hot,
Or the kitchen on a Sunday,
When Mum does the roast,
These are the smells I love the most!

Josie Bonnett (10)
St Paul's RC Primary School, Thames Ditton

THE HAMSTER POEM

Lovely and soft
Brown and white
Nice to handle
And he really won't bite
If you don't give him a fright.
He makes me giggle
And makes my dad frown
He's cuter than a mouse
Yes, you've got it right
He's my hamster
Sam!

Alexander Bellone (9)
St Paul's RC Primary School, Thames Ditton

MY CAT

In the morning when the fiery sun rises orange and bright
My snow white cat stretched her long legs one by one.
Then she jumps down off the chair she has been sleeping on.
I walk up to her and she walks through my legs,
Touching my cold legs with her warm fur.
She walks up to the door and looks at me with her soft dark eyes
And I open the door to the wide world for her to explore.
She walks through the alley onto the street where she finds a bin.
It has been knocked over so she decides to investigate the contents.
There in the back a mouse dangerously lingers nibbling on old cheese.
One look at my cat and she scurries down and hides in a small can.
So my cat scurries after her, searching but no luck.
Then she finds a nice shady place for a catnap under an oak
And sleeps, rolling over trying to catch her dreams as she purrs softly.
Then a ginger cat comes along, she's my cat's friend.
They play all day and when they've finished bouncing around
They sit side by side on a fence watching the sun go down
Purring softly.
I love my cat.

Lara Martin (11)
St Paul's RC Primary School, Thames Ditton

THE NIGHT

As the night began to fall
The night who I believe in came
I feel tired and alone when he comes
He is mystical and gentle
His face an invisible face
He has a spectacular embroidered coat
He moves smoothly and tucks me in.

Candice Wilson (11)
St Paul's RC Primary School, Thames Ditton

A TRANQUIL LIGHT

Transparent beams of glory protrude from the hilltops as
dawn approaches.
Like a phoenix had unleashed itself from beyond the mountains.
Life is born once more as immense rays of speed dominate
the wilderness.
Civilisation awakes to an empty day. Lifeless, an object of misery.
Like a vase with no flowers. A disco with no music. A comedian with
no audience.
The day staggers on. No flowers, no music, no comedy. No life.
Sorrow has punctured the hearts and souls of many. The wounds are
permanent.
Medicine is ineffective as they are just another form of destruction.
The exclusion of joy matches the well-being of none.
Life is not of the essence anymore, but survival.
The future has brought upon us fate. Death to joy. Death to a
tranquil light.

Josh Fenech (10)
St Paul's RC Primary School, Thames Ditton

SMELLS

Why is it that poets tell so little about the sense of smell?
There are the odours I love well:

The smell of bacon in a pan
Workman's tea in a can
The smell of petrol far away
Salty seas in the bay
The smell of boxes near to me
And the smell of my lovely tea
And the smell of the Sunday roast
There are the smells I love most.

David Ralph (9)
St Paul's RC Primary School, Thames Ditton

THE CIRCUS

The ringmaster yells at the top of his lungs,
Not much louder than vigorous tongues,
Clowns on stilts stand really tall,
Some start walking on a ball,
Tigers give their chops a lick,
Elephants show you their favourite trick,
Stuntmen juggle sticks of fire,
We hope they do not ever tire,
Men that swing on the scary trapeze,
They seem to do it with relentless ease,
Men juggle,
Kids get a cuddle,
People go in the tiger dome,
We wish we never had to go home,
It's so crowded you can hardly move in here,
But first we get a souvenir.

James Mullin (10)
St Paul's RC Primary School, Thames Ditton

THE NIGHT

A phantom dressed in a cloak of black
A demon rushing swiftly through the shadows
With a face of rage he moves from town to town
Dropping nightmares as he goes
Children fear him even in their sleep.

When his job is done he circles the sky
Laughing a terrible laugh
When the sun comes to take over the sky once again
He cowers back to his black castle
Beyond the dim clouds of the underworld.

Sebastian Whealing (11)
St Paul's RC Primary School, Thames Ditton

I'D RATHER BE . . .

I'd rather be a bat than a ball,
I'd rather be small than tall,
I'd rather be drinking Coke than Red Bull,
I'd rather be normal than cool,
I'd rather be Paul than Saul,
I'd rather be at rugby than football,
I'd rather be quick than stalled,
I'd rather be cool than a fool,
I'd rather be a floor than a wall,
I'd rather be fuel than a mule,
I'd rather be at football than the swimming pool,
I'd rather be a ball than rule,
I'd rather be Keenan than Kel.

Pearce Campion (10)
St Paul's RC Primary School, Thames Ditton

FORWARD THE LIGHT BRIGADE

Honour the Light Brigade
Honour the charge they made
Into the mouth of Hell they rode
Cannons on the left
Cannons on the right
Cannons in front of them coming into sight
Cannonball and shell flying around
While horse and hero fall to the ground
Honour the Light Brigade
Honour the charge they made
Noble six hundred

Anthony O'Loughlin (9)
St Paul's RC Primary School, Thames Ditton

I'D RATHER BE . . .

I'd rather be clean than smell.
I'd rather wear wax than gel.
I'd rather play a piano than a bell.
I'd rather be in Heaven than Hell.
I'd rather be called Anna than Mel.
I'd rather be C than L.
I'd rather be Keenan than Kel.
Id' rather be Rodney than Del.
I'd rather be in a cage than a cell.
I'd rather be naughty than tell.
I'd rather be crossed than parallel.
I'd rather do a sum than spell.
I'd rather buy than sell.
I'd rather be ill than well.
I'd rather be seaweed than a shell.
I'd rather make a cake than a spell.

Lawrence Fugle (10) & Michael Ellis (11)
St Paul's RC Primary School, Thames Ditton

THE MINISTER'S CAT

An angelic cat and her name is Angela
A ballerina cat and her name is Bella
A Chinese cat and his name is Ching Chang Chong
A dead cat and his name is Dontay
An exquisite cat and her name is Edwina
A flashy cat and her name is Felicity
A gangster cat and his name is Garry
A Hallowe'en cat and her name is Haunty
An Italian cat and her name is Italiano.

Freddie Gayle (10)
St Paul's RC Primary School, Thames Ditton

146

SMELLS!

Why is that poets tell
So little of the sense of smell?
These are the odours I love well . . .
The really strong perfume that my mum puts on
And the smell of a lovely baked icy bun.
The coffee that has been made for my mum,
I'm not allowed it but I'd love to have some.
The mint toothpaste when I clean my teeth
And the smell of the lovely baked roasted beef.
The odour of the crusty burnt toast.
These are the smells I love the most!

Louisa McCarthy (9)
St Paul's RC Primary School, Thames Ditton

WHAT CHRISTMAS MEANS TO ME

What Christmas means to me,
Read this poem and you will see.
Christmas is happiness and joy,
And it's all about Mary's baby boy.
The Three Wise Men who travelled afar,
To see Jesus born underneath a star.
We remember the people that live in the street,
And we forget how much food we get to eat.
That just leaves me one thing to say,
Enjoy the special *Christmas Day!*

Thomas Hewett (10)
St Paul's RC Primary School, Thames Ditton

I'D RATHER BE . . .

I'd rather be a bat than a ball
I'd rather climb than fall
I'd rather scream than call
I'd rather be small than tall
I'd rather walk than crawl
I'd rather be Bob than Saul
I'd rather go to nursery than school
I'd rather be big than small
I'd rather be happy than bawl
I'd rather be a fence than a wall
I'd rather be fungi than cool
I'd rather play snooker than pool
I'd rather be . . .

Chris Goldsmith (10)
St Paul's RC Primary School, Thames Ditton

I'D RATHER . . .

I'd rather be happy than sad.
I'd rather be mum than dad.
I'd rather be a lass than a lad.
I'd rather be Stan than Chad.
I'd rather be kind than mad.
I'd rather be good than bad.
I'd rather have than had.
I'd rather subtract than add.
I'd rather use a notebook than a pad.
0
Emily Lucas (11)
St Paul's RC Primary School, Thames Ditton

AS THE RAIN FALLS

As the rain falls
Someone quivers in the darkness,
Someone is waiting for a large thunderstorm,
The gloomy days go by one by one,
All life is cast away by shadows,
For all life was beautiful
But suddenly a curse,
Life will come back sometime.

Hannah Tookey (9)
St Paul's RC Primary School, Thames Ditton

THE STATIONARY TRAVELLER

The black box sat silently on the table,
What journey shall I go to, Sky or Cable?

I pushed the button and chose my path,
The sudden noises made me jump and laugh.

I'm a fan in the crowd at a football match,
With a flick of the button, I'm beamed into space with enemies to
despatch.

Later at Top of the Pops, I was doing some grooves,
Showing everyone my fantastic moves.

Then I departed my adventure, ended my day,
I just flicked off the TV and walked away . . .

Andrew Wright (10)
Salfords Primary School

DOGS

Cute and playful when a puppy,
Tired but sweet when old,
Fluffy ears and beady eyes.

Has lots of energy and fur,
Give it love and attention,
Fluffy ears and beady eyes.

All it needs is TLC
Also
Gives body protection when needed,
Fluffy ears and beady eyes.

Don't buy one for a Christmas present,
Unless you can look after it well,
Fluffy ears and beady eyes.

Michaela Bunt (11)
Salfords Primary School

DOG

Dangerous dodger,
Cocky character,
Rapid runner,
Cute cuddler,
Messy muncher,
Stealthy stealer,
Sleepy snorer,
Disgusting drooler.

Rhiannon Cass (9)
Salfords Primary School

MY FAVOURITE CAR

My favourite car is a Jaguar.
I don't know why, maybe it's because it's fabulous.
Maybe it's because they're powerful,
Or maybe it's luxurious.
It could be looks, it could be speed,
It could be special, or maybe it's just me.

The bodywork,
It's so fresh,
It's so clean,
To me it's supreme.
There are different types,
Different sounds.
It makes me wonder how they come up with all the different styles.

Richard Burrows (10)
Salfords Primary School

THE LONELY CAT

As the children are out to play,
Sleeps a cat at the bay,
Playing with the light on the wall,
Trying so hard not to fall.
His whiskers cold, his nose blue,
Every cat too -
Will do the same on Christmas Day,
Snuggled up beneath this sheet,
The lonely cat sleeps.

Iain Powell (11)
Salfords Primary School

UNDER THE SEA

There's a crystal palace under the waves,
Fish dance through pink weed and rocky caves,
Seaweed, plants of dark green and red,
Fish curl up snugly in their sandy bed.
There come the mermaids with brightly lit tails,
Then come the sharks, blue and white whales,
Jellyfish, starfish and all kinds of creatures,
Catfish, swordfish with all kinds of features.
The water lashes against the shore,
It sweeps the sand up off the floor,
Crystal and rock get washed by the tide,
The sea has lots of secrets deep inside,
You see there's magic beneath the blue,
Go see for yourself, you'll see it's true.

Cara Louise Hopkins (11)
Salfords Primary School

CHRISTMAS TREE

Your fairy lights shine so bright
Twinkling in the starry night
Making such a beautiful sight
For all the world to see
Such a beautiful Christmas tree.

The golden fairy on the top of our tree
Watches down on our family
As we open our presents with excitement and glee
Wondering what our surprises will be.

Jessica Stovell (10)
Salfords Primary School

152

WHAT IS YELLOW?

Yellow is a sunrise
Blazing and bright
Yellow makes you feel good
Yellow is a rotten leaf
Yellow is a bright colour
Yellow is a happy colour
The sun is a yellow beach ball kicked high
Into the summer sky
Yellow is a signal
That says: 'Get ready.'
Can you imagine living
Without yellow?
It would be very dull.

Simon Otah (10)
Sanderstead Junior School

LOVE

Love is beautiful,
And it's romantic.

Love is like the stars
In the sky
Twinkling in your eye.

If we never had
Love in the world,
The world would
Be an empty place.

Nicolle Williams (10)
Sanderstead Junior School

WHAT IS YELLOW?

Yellow is the sun,
Which glides over the land.
It is a lemon,
Which is very sour.
Yellow is very bright,
It cheers you up.
Yellow is a banana,
It is a kite,
It likes flying.
It is like a golden coin.
If there wasn't yellow,
The whole world would be dull.

Asuka Kumon (10)
Sanderstead Junior School

WATER

Water is in the seas
And in the streams
It flows gently
And calmly.
When it flows downwards
It ambushes the stones.
On the beach
Water grabs the sand
And drags it into the sea.
When water is angry
It drowns and destroys
Our homes and lives.

Anooj Thakrar (10)
Sanderstead Junior School

WHAT IS YELLOW?

Yellow is the sun,
Yellow is the sand,
Yellow is a daffodil
All beautiful and bright.
Yellow is a lemon
Which is rich but bitter.
Yellow is a coward
Who gets cheesed off.
Yellow is the yolk of
A slimy egg.
Yellow is the heat
Of a roaring fire.

What would the world be without yellow?
It would be dark and sunless.

Rakhee Kiran Shah (11)
Sanderstead Junior School

WHAT IS GREEN?

What is green? A field of fresh grass.
Green is cold, as cold as ice.
Green is the stem of a flower,
The leaves on a tree.
In summer green is everywhere,
It is everything you see.

The fruit on the tree is green,
Pears, apples and gooseberries.
But when winter comes,
All the green is gone.

Alex Forzani (10)
Sanderstead Junior School

A GHOST

A ghost is a sheet at night
On the washing line.
A ghost is a bag of water
Waiting to burst.
A ghost is a plastic bag
Blowing in the breeze.
A ghost is a shadow,
A ghost is a lost friend returning,
A ghost will make you shiver.
A ghost is a cool breeze.
A ghost is a thing you don't often see.

Lily Middleton (10)
Sanderstead Junior School

THE FOREST

I walked in a forest
One summer morning,
The giant trees towered high,
With a bright, gleaming sun,
Its light trickling through,
Dawning a new day.
I walked the whole day away,
Just wandering down the path,
Then thought about what the world
Was missing out on.

Persia O'Hara (11)
Sanderstead Junior School

THE RIVER

It starts in the hills,
as a little stream,
it trickles lazily,
going downhill.

It accelerates,
it crashes into stones,
getting wider and deeper,
as it runs.

Beginning to rush,
picking up the rocks,
splashing, eating away,
on its journey to the sea.

Slowing, slowing,
it virtually stops,
a delta forms.

At last the sea!

Rahul Bandopadhyay (9)
Sanderstead Junior School

WATER

Water runs from the hills,
Collecting things on its way,
Crashing stones to the ground,
It gradually eats away.

Water lets the fish go free,
It lets the boats go to sea,
Water lets the plants grow,
It makes the sea, it makes the snow.

Tim Freed (10)
Sanderstead Junior School

LIFE

Born baby
Scream from your mouth,
a bottle for a drink,
a cot just for you,
a song of love, with me and you,
a tear in your eye,
suddenly you start to cry.

Toddler
You play and laugh,
you have fun with your mum,
you start to talk,
then you walk,
then you write with pen and chalk,
you play all day.

Child
Then you wake and go to school.

Teenager
Steal from your mum,
swear and have fun,
get a job,
the fun has begun to fade.

Adult
Your life has begun,
say goodbye to the fun.

Old
You sleep all day,
and dream of what your life has been.
Goodbye friend,
it's the end!

Oliver Foley (10)
Sanderstead Junior School

THE FUTURE OF THE PLANET

Microsoft will have its own currency
It will be called the 'Gate'
Microsoft will provide everyone with a unicycle to transport themselves
For one reason and one reason only:
It is more economical
Microsoft will own the office in everyone's house
Because of a $10,000 purchase of Dos OS
Which has led to billions upon billions of dollars.
In the year 2001
Microsoft will own the living room in everyone's house
Because of something called
'XBox'
Seamus Blackley (aka Dr FeelGood) created the XBox
For one reason and one reason only:
World domination
For those unfamiliar with the XBox
It is a video game console, which will be available to purchase in 2001
For a rock bottom price of $300
It will have many goodies to come along with it such as a DVD player
and hard drive
XBox will come equipped with a limerick that goes like this:
'We all liked the Sony PlayStation
And the Dreamcast caused quiet a sensation
But when it comes to great games
Forget those other names
XBox is the next generation.'
All Microsoft needs to do next is conquer the bathroom.

George Yannimaras
The American School In England

INESCAPABLE DECLINE

Bite the hand that feeds you. Pigs rule.
Movements and rebellions only there to keep people occupied.

Everything moves in a loop. Empires press the self-destruct button.
Can't see their own downfall.

Media grips. News in, news out. The good news reaches people.
Just enough to stop progress.

Laws and rules restrict creativity. Society forces conformity.
Tells people how to think.

Children become parents, can't do what they want because of the dollar.
Make parents proud at graduation.

Everything overpriced. Just out of reach. Spend your life trying to get
something and then the price moves up.

The drill press of government and media. Every time a TV is switched
on, a newspaper opened, the drill moves in. Force ideas into people.

Rehab. Counselling. False security. Shield of lies.
Give some more money to corruption.

Hype towers over all. No one believes in anything enough to stand up
for it, only flags. Fists have a mind of their own.

Noting matters. Next pay check, next new product, next new child, next
new house, next new TV show.

Dreams wasted. Ideas gone. Give the responsibility to their kids.

Mardean Isaac
The American School In England

BOYS

Boys can be sweet but there is always a price to pay
Just when you think you have him
Your troubles are not far away
One day he is there
One day he is gone
So I'm warning any female out there
Stay away
Although we all say we will be aware

Once his cute eyes stare into yours
You're like a dog rolled over
Boys have a certain power
Once they take your hand
You are floating on top of the highest mountain
But everyone knows people can't fly
And you fall as fast as you rose
With only the scraps and bruises to show for
Although it seems the fall has killed you
Don't give up, this is just his first stage
His worst stage
As he gets older he will grow
Inside and out
He won't take you for any more meaningless rides
He will stay for a lifetime
You will share bad times along with good
Which will strengthen your relationship
So when you think there is no hope for him
And he will always be that way
Just know there is a bright future
When he becomes a man.

Alison Currie
The American School In England

161

WOMEN

Some women are like swans
    They are loyal to one and only one
    They return every year to the same old man
Some women are like bees
    They can't decide on one
    They flit from flower to flower without care
Some women are like flowers
    They bloom and wait for the one
    When he comes he leaves as fast as he came without a
        backwards glance
Some women are like butterflies
    They entice you with their wings
    But then you try to reach them they fly away
        But all women are one thing men always see
        They are lovely and loving and that's what they will always be.

Christian Griffin
The American School In England

BOYS AND GIRLS

Boys are like lime juice
They are extremely sour
They are like chocolate mousse
You take one bite and then devour

A boy is like a bottle of Coke
It is extremely sweet
A boy is unclear like a cloud of smoke
They make you feel complete

But boys are like a drink so fizzy
They are so unclear
They make your mind all dizzy
But girls are what they fear!

Lizzy Twining
The American School In England

BOOKS ARE BOYS

Boys are like books
They can be pretty slow
   at the beginning
But soon you can't
   put them down
Some are romantic, mysterious,
   some adventurous
And others that just make you
   crack up
Even if they look ugly and don't
   appeal on the outside
They can turn your world
   upside down
And make you see it differently
You can read them
over and
   over and
      over again
And never find the inside meaning
But soon they show you
   the meaning of life
Then you know you will
   keep it forever.

Alyson Cockerill
The American School In England

THE END OF THE WORLD

The end is near
The world is closing all around
I am spiralling through a pool of blackness
I can't hear any sound

I feel as though I'm flying
I am trembling with fear
I don't know where I'm headed
I know I must be near

Suddenly I am rushed into light
A spiral of white and black
I'm speeding through this maze of horror
And don't know when I'll be back

I wanted to say goodbye
Goodbye to Mom and Dad
And if you ever get this poem Alice
You're the sister I never had.

My breaths are getting shorter
So I must leave you now
I had hoped I would see you before the end
But I guess this is it all that's allowed.

Mom, Dad, I'm not scared any more
So please don't be for me,
I know I'll go on to a better place
I wish you two could see.

My own blood is all around me
I can hear the policeman say
'This girl's not going to make it,
Sadly there's no way.'

I only wish someone would have told him
Not to drink and drive
Because of his careless mistake
I had to pay with my life.

Michelle Ankrum
The American School In England

THEY

They tick like a bomb
They scold like my mum
Their hair smells like strawberries
Their nails ripe as raw cherries
They read lots of bookies
But hate boy-made cookies
You can play with them like those monkey toys
But then they bang they make lots of noise
In school they're bodacious
And act as if boys are brainless
At spending, they've got skills
But make men pay the bills
Their cooking is scrumpilicious
If you don't eat it they can be vicious
When they're in love they'll suck your blood
When you've got two they'll throw you in the mud
When they ask a question of you
Yes or no will just not do
They want you to be stylish with Armani and Gucci
So you don't look like a big sad poochie
Girls, girls, girls can make your heart hazy
But girls, girls, girls just make me crazy.

Manny Fassihi
The American School In England

ICE CREAM SCOOPS

Ice cream scoops with chocolate,
That's the way they should be;
Or with fresh strawberries,
That's the way I like them for me.
But sometimes the ice cream is too cold,
Or all soft and mushy.
And sometimes they have little bits,
Of chocolate or sprinkles:
The trick is not to have too much.
If you leave it out too long, it melts away,
Wasted, never tastes as good again.
And there are flavours for different types,
One for every person in the world.
A lot of people like chocolate,
Even more like vanilla,
But some like pistachio or even hazelnut,
Others like strawberry.
Various tastes are rambunctious or sweet,
Or even bitter or crazy.

Caroline Troein
The American School In England

THE FUTURE OF OUR PLANET

Curing diseases we thought incurable;
Advances in the field of technology;
Using only energy efficient methods;
This is the future of our planet.

Worldwide tolerance of religion;
Elimination of all prejudices;
Peace and tranquillity at all times;
This is the future of our planet.

Viewing everything positively;
Understanding the value of a life;
Appreciating the blessings one possesses;
This is the future of our planet.

Megan Wright
The American School In England

BOYS AND PHOTOGRAPHS

Both photos and boys can be beautiful,
At first glance they are perfect
You can't find anything wrong
But then you realise
Even though they are the perfect souvenirs
They don't show any emotion
Both seem to mask what's really going on
That picture of the snow-topped mountain
Looks exactly like it did that day
But
Then you remember what really happened that day
That boy is perfect
They're all a boy should be
You know them as well as humanly possible
Sorry
You don't
At least not until they take off their masks
The masks that shield their inner beauty
Both boys and photos are beautiful
Only with the joy they bring to you
When they show themselves
Their true selves.

Marika Bigler
The American School In England

A TIME TOO NEAR

This dying planet that we live upon is becoming older every day
And yet many pay no mind
Because the present is where we stay
The future will just pass behind
Some notice our harmful ways
They understand that our habit pays
I sometimes wonder who the world will be
With an older different me
Although we may come up with new plans
And more food will be available in cans
What we need what will someday be is action
Too many people are preoccupied with relaxation
Our air may not be quite as pure
We may have found a brand new cure
But of this I am sure
Our civilisation will remain the same
We will continue to cause more acid rain
Our sky will turn ever darker shades of grey
More waste will kill animals in the nearby bay
Our wasted time kills unborn prey
The time that we await,
The time that is never here,
The future that becomes the past,
The future that will never arrive,
Is coming all too soon.

Ben Machado
The American School In England

THOSE GIRLS

Those girls, always got a secret to tell,
Those girls, never give clues to ring any bells,
Those girls, know everything that's going on,
Those girls, might hate you or love you a ton,

Those girls, talking behind your back,
Those girls, always wanting a guy with a six pack,
Those girls, always secretive and closed up,
Those girls, wearing fifty layers of make-up.

Andrew Livanos
The American School In England

BOYS

There are all kinds of boys -
Boys who are bossy -
Boys who are sly -
Boys who will listen -
Boys who don't cry.

The boys who will tease -
The boys who will not -
Joking and jesting -
Hoping not to get caught.

Boys and their hobbies -
Are different from girls -
Buzz, squish, pop, zing
Versus ribbons and curls.

Their heart's made of stone -
Some stubborn as a mule's -
They sometimes think -
They are quite cool.

Boys can be friends -
Above all the rest -
Honest and reliable -
No need to impress!

Paige Bryant
The American School In England

THE PLANET EARTH

Mother Earth is dying slowly
like a patient with cancer
she is crying tears of sorrow
bang, boom, bang
war is happening everywhere
killing people and destroying the
landscape of the Earth
the flag at half mast
now lies on the ground
for
there is
no
government
and
the
world is
governed by
rebels without a
cause
death, dying and destruction
everywhere
the Earth is a
bomb
ticking
towards its end.

Chris Drakopoulos
The American School In England

GIRLS

They know every shortcut and secret,
They're there to hold your hand or they're with your best friend,
But they always know the way out and always find the light,
90% right and when you're wrong the world has ended,
But when they're wrong it's, 'Oh I'm sorry,'
Yes, it's the ones who wake up and don't know what to wear,
Sometimes it's, 'Oh I have to look right,'
Others it's just a ponytail,
Oh yes, some of them care,
But others, well, who the heck cares?
Sometimes they're the devil's best friend, planning and plotting,
And other times they have a halo over their head,
Yes, the nail-painters, the ones with special designs,
And oh yes, the girls, the million pairs of shoes,
Every colour, style and groove.

Mike Millstein
The American School In England

WHY IS BLUE SO BLUE?

There once was a dog named Blue,
Who had friends exactly two,
They were Shovel and Pail,
And got eaten by a whale,
And that's why Blue is so blue.

Alex Latimer
The American School In England

THE NEXT GENERATION

What will we leave
For the next generation,
Solutions,
Or problems,
Or half-shared truths?

Gaps,
Holes,
Leaks,
Pollution,
Natural or man-made,
Are we sure?
Invention takes us beyond the present
But potentially creates future legacies from the past.

Inter-galactic communication,
Destination,
Unknown,
Black holes,
Particle matter,
A start or a finish?

Evolution,
Gods or genetics,
Religion,
War,
Peace,
Faith,
Spirits or souls?

Diversity of colour,
Race or creed,
Community spirit,
Human challenge,
Political answers or half-shared commitments,
Do we mean it or do we not?

What will we leave
For the next generation,
Solutions,
Or problems,
Or half-shared truths?

Beth Lloyd-Jones
The American School In England

GIRLS

All girls are like rivers
Some flow fast, others move slowly
But they're always moving
Some rivers are shallow but most rivers are deep
And unless you look really hard, you never see the bottom
Some rivers' courses can be changed
Others are stubborn and stuck up following a predetermined course
Some rivers are short and windy following paths that often change
The best thing about rivers are their waterfalls
Some are surging and powerful
Others are peaceful and mellow and have
   Small rocks smoothed over the flow of time which
      Makes their paths longer to reach you but makes
         Them so special you want to capture them in a picture
But like girls when rivers get old they never lose their beauty
Some still surge the way they used to
Other seem calmer and more fluent
   And you know what?
   I like rivers.

Reed Gilbert
The American School In England

POEM

Toys and girls are alike
You want a certain type so bad
That you would do nearly anything to get it
When you get it at first you have lots of fun with it
But like any other toy it starts to get boring
And you want a new toy.

Jason Meyer
The American School In England

GIRLS

Girls are like a golf game,
You're always chasing and never winning,
Girls are like a window,
Opening and closing as they please.

Preston Nelson
The American School In England

WHAT HAVE WE DONE?

Black darkness, choking.
Wheezing . . . Coughing . . . Gasping . . . Gone.
Gone like hope and dreams.

Lauren Scott
The American School In England

GIRLS AND DOGS

Girls are a lot like dogs
There are different types, different sizes, and different attitudes
Little, twitchy girls are like chihuahuas
And big, mean girls are like pit bulls
Although the types vary, they all love to be with each other
And love to be loved
Yet they can and do snap at strangers
It would be hard to live in this world without them
They can be loyal, or they can try to run away
Boys are always trying to get one
However, sometimes they don't like their boy
They can be so unpredictable
They can kiss, love, like, dislike, hate, bite
But boys keep looking for and loving them
Girls are a lot like dogs.

Richard Nickson
The American School In England

BOYS

A boy is like a cat.
They lounge around all day in the sun,
Just sitting and sleeping
With an occasional run.
When they see something they just can't live without,
They purr and they plea day in and day out.
When they finally get what they are after
They're content, they're happy with occasional laughter.
Despite their bad habits
And despite their bad lies
What would we do without cats in our lives?

Emily Koch
The American School In England

GIRLS

Girls are like cars
Some are loud and some
Are quiet
But they all drive you round the bend

Some are old
A few are new
Some you hate
But some are built
Just for you

Every once in a while
Or quite frequently
You trade one in for another
But someday you'll find one
You'll never want to lose.

Laurence Ungless
The American School In England

BOYS

Boys are like snow
You wait for days on end for the perfect one to come
Yet when it finally does, it seems to go just as fast
Then there's times when it comes
And you find out it's not the right type
There are times when you find it just plain annoying
But then there's the perfect type
The type of snow you want to build snowmen with
Just like the type of guy you have always wanted
Boys are like snow.

Casey Clark
The American School In England

THE EARTH

Will the
Earth's future be
As happy as we would
Like it to be. Or will it be
Dark and scary, some people
May think 'on the contrary'. Will
The little birdie sing while it's perched
On the tree. Will the tree even be there
Or will all we do is stare, stare,
Stare? Will the ground that it is
In be there at all or be very
Thin. All that we can
Do is wonder and
Think. The
Future.

Kevin McAlister
The American School In England

GIRLS ARE LIKE THE SUN

Girls are like the sun
Beautiful, the centre
Of the universe, but
Get too close
You shall die instantly!
Blocked from love.
The heat and gas,
Like a rejection,
Horrible to even think of.
Girls are like the sun.

Jonathan Prinsell
The American School In England

GIRLS

Girls are like yachts.
The two best days of a man's life,
Are when he gets one, and when he loses one.
If you get one,
Your best friend's is always better,
And once you get the best,
A better one suddenly appears.
The best of them all look so great on the outside,
But once you get to know the interior, its value plummets.
But there is always the one,
The overlooked, the perfect,
The one that is worthless to others,
But everything in the world to you.

Andrew Krutz
The American School In England

MY BROTHER

Justin is like a slimy slug
Just sits around all day
Leaves his slimy trail behind him
And doesn't bother to pick up after himself
He has always done this unique habit
And will always do it
But even worse than ever
Like complaining about school, homework and reading

Though on the outside he may be sluggish
But inside he is sweet and soft
He can be sluggish and childish a times
But I love him, he's my brother.

Kaitlin Przezdziecki
The American School In England

GIRLS

Girls are like basketballs.
Always bouncing and bouncing until you control them from the
commotion.
If you don't make your move fast enough
You don't score the point,
And another player will steal the ball,
And if it is stolen you just have to wait for your next pass
Because who knows what is going to happen next?
Girls are like basketballs.
Unpredictable.
You never now what the score is going to be.
Even after all the pain you suffer
You come to realise,
Basketball
Is your passion inside.

Tim Lynch
The American School In England

GIRLS

Girls are like shops in a mall.
There are so many to choose from
But only one has what you're looking for.
You browse all day trying to find the right one
And when you see the store that you know is right
You go straight to it.
But when you're inside the other shops look better
And at the end of the day when you know which shop is the best
You go back to it and it is closed
So you have to wait for it to open again.

Charles Tyler
The American School In England

OUR NEW PLANET

Our new planet will be
starstruck for eternity

With no mountains or plateaux to see
when the skies are level to the ocean sea

When the stars shine bright
during the burning night

The only animals around
are those sleeping underground

All is quiet
no one is near

This is our new planet
no need to fear.

Lindsey Schortman
The American School In England

SOME GIRLS

Some girls are hot
Some girls are not
Some girls are nice
Some girls have life
Some girls are down
Some girls are like clowns
Some girls are tall
Some girls are small
Some girls are like bees
Some girls are perfect to *me.*

Will Meyer
The American School In England

MOTHER EARTH

The gales of the future
have swept you away
and you have vanished into
the black hole of sin
Pollution has choked out
your last breath
Now you are falling
down, down, deep into
eternity
Oh Mother Earth,
the place of human chaos,
I wish you could tell me
what went wrong.

Missy Gandy
The American School In England

FUTURE

In the future
The world will be dark

In the future
We will be on Mars

In the future
The air will be dirty

In the future
Our children will grow with pollution

In the future
We will all be gone.

Nicole Kereszti
The American School In England

BOYS

Boys can be tall
Boys can be small
Boys can run through the hall
They splish
They splash in the puddles
Causing all sorts of troubles
Boys are like trains, moving as fast as they can
They can be friends
They can be annoying
They can be nice also mean
Boys can be happy
Boys can be sad
Most of all
Boys aren't too bad!

Emma Musgrave
The American School In England

BOYS

Boys are like the wind.
Sometimes they can be rough and hard.
Sometimes they can be soft and kind.
Boys are like the sun.
They can be harsh and hurtful.
And sometimes they can be gentle and chase away the cold.
Boys can be like snow.
They can be cold and sting.
But they can be soft and fun.

That's what boys are.

Kay Froelich
The American School In England

GIRLS

I said I would always love you,
Even if you didn't care.
I said I would always want you,
You and your lovely streams of hair.
We'd walk down beaches with endless conversations.
We'd never have any confrontations.
We'd love and care and hold each other tight.
You'd never be lonely another night.

If grew up and moved away,
In my heart you'd always stay.
No other girl could take your place,
No other could equal your pretty face.
We'd care for each other in thickness and in thin,
You are my only love within . . .

Ben G
The American School In England

MENU OF THE FUTURE EARTH

Today on the menu for the planet Earth,
Is a large polluted piece of hearth.
Just like a pig sty in the Old McDonald's farm,
Then add some global warming which will do no harm.
The Earth will be *green* with envy,
And cry and cry boo hoo all day,
Because all the other planets have a better menu for the month of May!
I wonder what the future Earth will have in store,
We'll just have to wait until we walk right through that door.

Allison Ghegan
The American School In England

THE FLAME THAT NEVER WENT OUT

Still till this day that very same flame
That Jesus lit is still burning for peace,
For love, for joy, for our lives we still pray.
The flame is burning this minute, this second, this hour,
Will it ever go out or will it stay lit?
Jesus is still watching the flame burn
As the days, months, years pass by.
Every day it's a new start to life
Let's hope that the flame will stay lit forever.

Rustie Treagus (11)
Walton On The Hill Primary School

CANDLES

C   olourful candles shining brightly on a window shelf.
A   lmost every second molten wax is coming down.
N   ever put your hands on them, they will get burnt.
D   ecorative candles melt extremely quickly.
L   ight candles with extreme caution.
E   veryone can get burnt.
S   ometimes they hiss and spit! So beware!

Alex Mackworth-Praed (10)
Walton On The Hill Primary School

THE CANDLE

The candle was flickering in the night making the room glow bright.
It made me feel warm and cosy and it made my cheeks rosy.
It melted down all the way round until it fell to the ground.
The room smelt of wonderful scents, not bad, it only cost 50 pence.

Luke Bennett (10)
Walton On The Hill Primary School

MY NAUGHTY NEIGHBOUR

My naughty neighbour is such a pain
She washes spiders down the drain.
When she looks over the fence
I feel so deadly tense.
My naughty neighbour is over 10 feet tall
And just loves playing football.
My naughty neighbour is so divine
And just loves drinking wine.
She gets drunk
And turns into a punk
And funks all night till she drops dead on the floor.
Then when she's not doing that
She goes for a swim in our swimming pool.

Gemma Spicer (10)
Walton On The Hill Primary School

MY LITTLE DOG

My little dog is black and white.
He comes out at night,
To give us a fright.
My little dog is cute as can be.
He sits by the tree,
Until it's time for his tea.
He does his best to be good,
But when it's time for his pud
He runs off in the wood.
The moon is shining in the sky
On my little dog called Pie.
When he comes out he tells loads of lies
To the dragonflies.

Mark Spicer (10)
Walton On The Hill Primary School

THE BIG DREAM

One winter's day I lay in bed
With different thoughts all in my head,

I dreamed about all different things
From twinkling stars and submarines,
Well after that I came so near
Then suddenly I disappeared.

Well I went to school that very same day
I saw my teacher floating by
Into the deep dark wondrous sky.

The next thing that I knew
I found myself wandering to outside space
I started sweating and became very hot
But then I found myself speeding down a rock.
I wandered back to this strange black door
To find myself in a pack of four
I stood on something close to me
And realised it was my mummy.

I focused and I focused
My eyes went to a beam,
Then I realised this was all a dream.

Charlotte Smith (11)
Walton On The Hill Primary School

THE MOUSE ON HIS JOURNEY

There is a mouse
Who lives in a hole
He comes out
To climb the pole
To get the cheese
He sees the cat
And hits him with a baseball bat

He gets to the top of the pole
And gets past all of the traps
And goes, 'Hooray!
I got the cheese
Now let's go home
And share it with my family.'

Andrew Farrington (10)
Walton On The Hill Primary School

WHAT IS BLUE?

Blue is the colour
of my brand new car
Blue is the flowers
growing in the woods
Blue is the flame leaping
from open fire
Blue is the blanket
that keeps me warm
Blue is the star
shining from afar
Blue is the umbrella
where I hide from the rain
Blue is the sea
glittering in the sun
Blue is the sky
on a summer's day
Blue is the bird flying
up, up high
Could you do without *blue?*

Ben Cox (10)
Walton On The Hill Primary School

WHAT DO YOU WANT TO BE WHEN YOU GROW UP?

What do you want to be when you grow up?
You could be an astronaut
and shoot off in a rocket
You could be a jeweller
and make a gold locket

You could be a nurse
and patch up someone's knee
You could be a waitress
and serve people tea

You could be a banker
and store everyone's money
You could be a clown
and look really funny

You could be a chef
and make a cake
You could be a robber
and take, take, take

What do you want to be when you grow up?

Victoria Stephenson (11)
Walton On The Hill Primary School

AUTUMN

Slowly, drifting the crisp leaves fall,
Orange, brown and yellow,
The nights grow longer
And the days turn chilly and mellow.

The animals prepare for their winter hibernation,
Collecting nuts and berries,
So when they wake up in the springtime,
They'll be full of food and merry.

The wind blows gently and rustles all the leaves,
It blows your hair into your face so you cannot breathe,
It whips the branches of the trees,
So they bend and break with ease.

Hannah Turnbull (11)
Walton On The Hill Primary School

POP BANDS

There are many pop bands in the world,
Some are hot and some are cold,
What the heck, I don't care,
Most of them have hair and flair.

My favourite pop band is S Club 7,
They look really cool in lots of denim.
I wonder if the girls are in love,
Or just a sign from peace from above.

If pop bands can really sing,
What's the use of a ping, ping, ping,
Can they really sing a lar or is it just
A par in one?

Are the rumours really true,
Or is it just a fact from you?
See them perform with a stand,
How many pop bands are there?
(Really I don't care.)

Once I heard that pop bands can't sing,
I was devastated but couldn't give a ring a ling ding.

What's the use of pop bands if they can't sing a lar or a ping,
Really I don't care as long as I have a song to sing.

Stephanie Giles (11)
Walton On The Hill Primary School

ICE

Ice is that feeling, when petrified of the immortal,
It is that vigorous and despicable evil that haunts the world.
Ice is that unpredictable misfortune that everybody experiences.
It is the white in the Union Jack, irritably freezing the country.
Ice is what lies ahead of you when you have sinned.
It is a whimsical prison, capturing the good and freeing the bad.
Ice is that force, which is impressionable upon evil, which is the force
that values its existence.
It is a foe, that bring sorrow to many.
Ice makes people suffer, and makes people hate.
It is a demon, that surreptitiously forces you to do wrong.
Ice is a mass murderer, wanted by all, except for its followers, who seek
power and to be feared and want to have all unimportant qualities.

Alex Romaines (11)
Walton On The Hill Primary School

HOME TIME

Home time in our class is always a rush,
Children shouting, teacher, 'Hush now, hush.'
Children handing in their work and tidying the table,
Except that is for Tom, Jessica, Fiona and Mabel.

Tidying up the classroom, scissors in their drawer,
Everyone is sitting up straight, ready to go out of the door.
Handing out of homework, handing out of a letter,
'Class, hoods up, really the weather gets wetter and wetter.'

With their hoods up everyone goes hurrying outside,
Ready to play on the park's brand new, red slide.
Just as they leave teachers says, 'Goodbye,'
When they get home, Mother says, 'Hi.'

Claire Eggar (11)
Walton On The Hill Primary School

GRANNY'S FIRST FLIGHT

Granny's at the checkout
Her face as white as chalk
She's never flown away before
And all she does is talk.

She's telling everybody
How brave she's going to be
And all about the other time
The time she went by sea.

'Never flown before,' she said
'Never in all my life.
But as we fly
I'll close my eyes,
Small prayers inside my head
Repeat,' she said.

Laura Sharkey (11)
Walton On The Hill Primary School

THE HAUNTED HOUSE

Once as I was coming home from school,
I saw a house with a stream and a pool,
I went right up to the gate post,
And suddenly I saw a ghost,
It came right up, it looked at me,
I think it's a pirate from the sea,
I gave a scream,
It jumped in the stream,
I gave a cough,
Its leg fell off,
And I never saw him again.

Rachel Garrett (10)
Walton On The Hill Primary School

THE FOOTBALL GAME

A is for Always being fit for the game,
B is for Best performance or you'll get the blame.
C is for Champions, they all want to be,
D is for Defeated, we'll just have to see.
E is for Eleven, the players on the field,
F is for Friendly, the friendship is sealed.
G is for Goalie, he must try to catch,
H is for Hat trick, the man of the match.
I   is for Injury, you never know when,
J   is for Jumping, and trying again.
K is for Kick off, the game has begun,
L   is for Linesman, up and down he must run.
M is for Manager, a telling off never hurt,
N is for Number you wear on your shirt.
O is for Opposition, they keep you on the run,
P is for Penalty, they try to score one.
Q is for Quickness, you just have to try,
R is for Result, a win or a tie.
S is for Striker, he's the best chance we've got,
T is for Tactics, he uses a lot.
U is for United, now the minutes are up,
V is for Victorious, we hold up the cup.
W is for whistle, we all give a cheer,
X is for Xmas, we'll be back next year.
Y is for Youth we'd all like to redeem,
Z is for Zealous, so eager and keen.

Jamie Simmons (10)
Walton On The Hill Primary School

THE MOUSE CHASE

Warming in the sun, eyes blinking fast,
A mouse is always wondering about the past.
Nose twitching, ears alert,
A mouse is always ready for a very quick spurt.

Snoring and yawning,
There should always be a warning.
Cat a creeping, smelling,
Looking for the mouse's dwelling.

Searching for a furry mouse
Perhaps this could be its little house.
Found him, got him,
Ahhhh, lost him.

Mouse panting, sweating, dripping
Hearing the curtains torn by the cats ripping.
Hissing and snarling the cat pauses,
Is that better than a starling?

Sprinting and running
The mouse holds its breath
Expecting its impending death.

Home at last it's gone too fast,
Ready for bed.
Tossing and turning,
Now for safety a mouse is always yearning.

Frances Kenyon (11)
Walton On The Hill Primary School

FLU

Boiling hot,
  Icy cold,
    Runny nose,
      Sore throat.

Head spinning,
  Eyelids closing,
    Tossing, turning,
      Shouting, screaming.

Bad dreams,
  Cold sponge,
    Makes no sense,
      Medicine spoons.

Getting better,
  Cosy sweater,
    Comfy sofa,
      Hot soup.

Get well letters,
  TV programmes,
    Warm blankets,
      Soft tissues.

Feeling better,
  Take off sweater,
    Lots of sleep,
      Must do homework!

Gemma Brogan (10)
Walton On The Hill Primary School

BIRTHDAYS

The best birthday I've ever had
Wasn't with my brother. I'm glad!
It was when I was eleven,
And I invited Jordan and Stefan.

When I was only eight,
My birthday was with the brother I hate.
We went to the Spectrum - ice skating -
But all I did was stand hesitating.

The best birthday I've ever been to
Would have to be Jenna's - at the zoo!
We saw the monkeys and the apes,
When they fed them, they gave them grapes.

Ben Thomas (11)
Warren Mead Junior School

FAVOURITE PLACE - UNDER MY BEDCOVERS!

No one can come in because it's private.
No one can come in because it's secret.
Under my bedcovers, I'm so dozy,
Under my bedcovers, I'm so cosy.
No room for seating,
But it has heating.
Little bears next to me,
Fallen asleep next to me . . . next to me . . . next to me.
Goodnight!
Sleep tight!

Sally Fletcher (10)
Warren Mead Junior School

WORST BIRTHDAY

I know birthdays are supposed to be fun,
But think of the times when they can go wrong!
Everything's planned and everyone comes,
Even the troublemakers invited along.
You couldn't wait!
Suddenly people push through the door,
Don't hesitate.
All they say is 'Hello' and no more.

In comes a group not even polite,
Run through the door and then start a fight.
Mum's china is broken,
Trophies smashed on the floor!
Dad's cigars smoken
Troublemakers soon bore.

Into the dining room
Grab all the food
Someone yells, *'Boom!'*
Mum disappears in a mood.

Jelly's thrown in your face,
Someone lets out a scream
'Stop! It's a disgrace!'

Looks at all, who are seen.
'Get out of my house!
Don't bother to moan!
You've spoilt both my party
And my home!'

They run to the door
And I start to cry,
There's food on the floor,
Mum returns, wipes my eye,
'Don't worry darling, it'll soon be all right,
We'll clean this mess up before it is night!'

Christina Davis (11)
Warren Mead Junior School

MY FAVOURITE THINGS

My favourite place to sit,
Is in the conservatory,
It's cosy and warm and brightly lit,
In the conservatory.

My favourite time of day,
Is at around four o'clock.
It's sunny and light and time to play
At around four o'clock.

My favourite view of hills.
Is the vast view down my road.
It's peaceful and quiet and always still,
The view down my road.

My favourite pets I have kept,
Are my dog and two black cats.
They're lively and fun and have never slept.
My dog and two black cats.

Elizabeth Thompson (9)
Warren Mead Junior School

POEM ON BIRTHDAYS

Center Parcs was quite amazing
Cycling, bowling, swimming, skating.
The swimming pool with all those slides,
I was in for a huge surprise!
Little did I know it
But all my friends had made a plot.
A chocolate cake for all to see,
was sitting waiting, just for me!

The animal park was long and wide,
We went on the trailer for a ride,
To see the animals they had there.
A gorilla gave us quite a scare,
By banging on the cages
And going into rages.
The day, it ended, we were in the car,
Now we had to travel far.

The swimming party was a great success
My sister wore a lovely dress,
Of pink and white, red that glistened,
Not one single person listened
To what I had to say,
They were all busy singing Happy Birthday!
I'm growing older, next I'm twelve,
I keep all my presents on my shelves.

Hayley Javeleau (11)
Warren Mead Junior School

NIGHT-TIME!

It's night-time!
Mum's turned out the light,
It's night-time!
And she's said goodnight,
It's night-time!
I can go to sleep,
And I wish that I could keep,
Asleep!

It's night-time!
And I'm in despair,
It's night-time!
'Cause it's time for night-time scare.
It's night-time!
And I wish that I could stay
Asleep!

It's morning!
And mum's come to wake me up,
It's morning!
And my dream it went 'Kah-put!'
It's morning!
My wish did not come true to stay
Asleep!

Tom Bovington (10)
Warren Mead Junior School

BIRTHDAYS

I woke up in the morning,
Feeling special deep down.
When I came out of my bedroom,
There was no -one around.

I crept downstairs
And everyone was there,
With a huge pile of presents,
I could feel their care!

On another occasion
It was not mine,
To tell you the truth,
It was a disastrous time!

Lying in bed was my poor old dad,
I must admit I was there too,
I could not help thinking I'd spoilt his birthday,
I had given him the flu.

Sara Manaton (11)
Warren Mead Junior School